THE PROPHECIES OF
NOSTRADAMUS

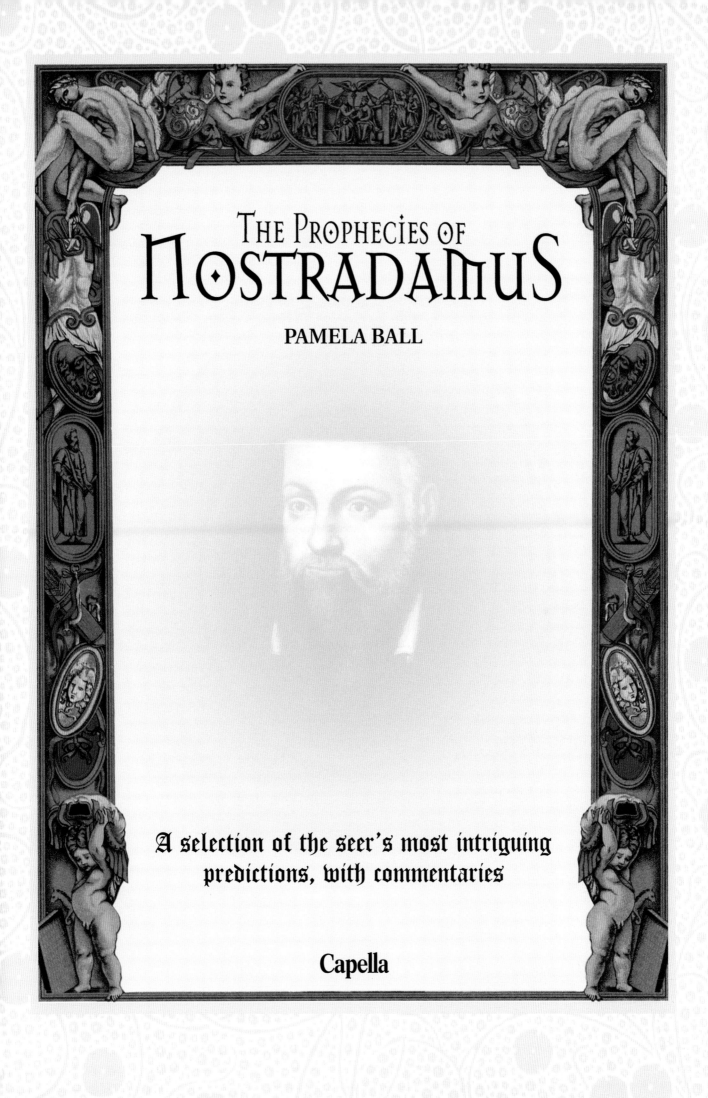

The Prophecies of NOSTRADAMUS

PAMELA BALL

A selection of the seer's most intriguing
predictions, with commentaries

Capella

This edition published in 2005 by Arcturus Publishing Limited
26/27 Bickels Yard, 151–153 Bermondsey Street,
London SE1 3HA

In Canada published for Indigo Books
468 King St W,
Suite 500,
Toronto,
Ontario M5V 1L8

ISBN 1-84193-329-5

Printed in China

Cover Design: Steve Flight
Art Director: Beatriz Waller
Design: Laura Casella
Thanks to *The Grammar of the Ornament* by Editore Gremese,
for some of the decorative images

Contents

Introduction

ny author who sets out to explore the work, the life or the times of the man now known as Nostradamus steps into a minefield of opposing beliefs, claim and counterclaim. Probably as much of an enigma today as when he lived, he offers us insights and information as he perceives them and expects us to follow him in his reasoning and in the way he works. It behoves us therefore to get to know the man, his work and the hopes and fears he had.

When considering Nostradamus' writings one cannot help but feel that he must have been something of a genius to have been able to calculate the timings of his predictions in the way that he did. He was a skilled astrologer of some repute at a time when astrology held somewhat more weight than it does today. It would be wonderful to feel that we could have access to all his different methods of calculation. The ability to use computers has enabled modern mathematicians to replicate his calculations and given us reasonable proof that he was generally accurate.

Nostradamus, the man

Michel de Nostradame was born in the city of Saint-Remy, in Provence, France 'in the year of our Lord 1503, on Thursday, December 14, around noon'. Nostradamus came from a long line of Jewish doctors and scholars and he is

said to have begun his studies at his grandfather's knee. His family had converted from Judaism to Christianity in 1502, as a result of persecution on the ascension of Louis XII, and it would be interesting to speculate whether his family had an interest in Jewish mysticism and Kabbalah. The name 'de Nostradame' (of Our Lady) may have been chosen deliberately to signify the use of the intuitive arts as well as the new allegiance to the Catholic Madonna. It was only later in life that our seer chose to use the more masculine form.

His education was a fairly liberal one and this is shown in many of his quatrains which use numbers of classical references and demonstrate a considerable knowledge. Opinions vary as to whether he actually studied medicine, but he was certainly a healer before he began writing and his views on hygiene and herbalism became widely appreciated during the time of the Black Death.

His healing ability was to be his greatest burden, however, for the plague killed Nostradamus' wife and two children, whom he adored. The fact that he was unable to save his own family had a disastrous effect on his practice and, one presumes, on his state of mind. Shortly after her death his wife's family tried to sue him for the return of her dowry, and the final straw came in 1538 when he was accused of heresy. Ever the wanderer, he chose to evade the authorities and travelled widely. It is probable that in this period, about which we know little, he incorporated much learning and developed further his interest in alchemy and the related arts.

By 1554 Nostradamus had settled in Marseilles. In November that year, Provence experienced one of the worst floods of its history, with its attendant sicknesses. Subsequently, Nostradamus moved on to Salon, and in the November he married Anne Ponsart Gemelle, a rich widow. Here, he decided to write his *Prophéties*, and the first incomplete set were circulated probably in 1555.

In 1556 he was summoned to the court of Henri II and Catherine de Medici, the latter being extremely interested in his work, and employed him to calculate the astrological charts of her seven children. From that time on, under her patronage, his fame spread and he continued with his work.

Shortly before his death in 1566 he left instructions as to the disposal of his body, requesting that he be buried in an upright position in the wall of the local church. On 1 July he sent for the local priest and told his assistant that he would not see him alive again. He was found the next morning in exactly the position he had predicted.

His works

Nostradamus began his major work early in 1554, seemingly in response to a series of omens after publishing a number of almanachs in the four years previously. He used the form of the quatrain, a type of verse that is quite brisk and straightforward. It consists of four lines, normally rhyming AB AB, though this sometimes forces Nostradamus to take liberties with language.

He also gives us a handy way of categorizing his quatrains without necessarily recognizing that he has done so. Many people like to think that his words in his first two quatrains about the tripod signify the Past, the Present and the Future and it seems sensible to take those three periods of time to begin our exploration.

Obviously, because he was domiciled in France his first concern was for that country, but in this book for the section on the past we have deliberately decided not to include those quatrains which are particularly focused on that country, except for one. That is the one which Nostradamus is believed to have written as the alternative to Century X Quatrain 100 which forecasts the coming of the Sun King Louis XIV.

There is a saying something to the effect that the past creates the present and the present gives birth to the future. In the section on our present day, which we have defined as the last one hundred years, we confess that we have not verified the calculations, going for a much more intuitive viewpoint in order to offer some interpretations of his more startling quatrains. We have divided the section up into those quatrains dealing with royalty, those dealing with religious changes, with war (a favourite subject of Nostradamus) and others which have a political sheen or are somewhat contentious.

In trying to understand us and the way in which we will live in the future, Nostradamus would not have been able to rely on his usual symbolism, but would have had to invent almost a new way of thinking to accommodate his perception. Hence he will speak of 'a dart from the sky' or 'a swamp of crystal'. His images are very evocative and perhaps therefore the more disturbing or thought provoking for being so.

Nostradamus must have been well aware of the effect that his work would have on people. Cleverly, in an effort to remain one step ahead of his detractors at a time of persecution, he pays lip service to anyone who may be trying to catch him out as an occultist. He admits that as he suspects his knowledge may at some point be called into question, he has himself 'destroyed' his source of knowledge. But who knows how much he has committed to memory?

In a letter to his son César he has told us what he has done to protect himself. He writes:

Although such occult philosophy might not have been condemned, I had no desire to make freely public all its unbridled assertions. I had at my disposal several volumes that had been hidden for a great many centuries.

But dreading what might otherwise become of them I made a present of them to Vulcan and even as he began to consume them, his hungry flame lent the air an unusual brightness, clearer than that of natural flame – bright as lightning – suddenly illuminating the house as if in a sudden conflagration.

Vulcan was a Roman fire-god, particularly associated with destructive fire. Denied access to Mount Olympus, he fashioned a forge in the heart of Mount Etna and is said to have created a golden throne for the goddess Juno, as well as fashioning Jupiter's magical thunderbolts and Cupid's arrows.

Nostradamus indicates that in burning his magical books he actually achieves that moment of 'clear light' – total clarity of perception – that all alchemists hope for in their search for knowledge.

Nostradamus' hidden message here is that without alchemical and magical knowledge – and perhaps a little assistance from the gods – there cannot be a full understanding of what he is setting forth. However, he later goes on to say that by careful calculation his prophecies can be checked.

Nostradamus was often, we suspect, trying to warn people that if they did not mend their ways what he saw was inevitable. He in his own way therefore attempted to get closer to God.

EFFIGIES TYCHONIS BRAHE O.F.
ÆDIFICII ET INSTRUMENTORUM
ASTRONOMICORUM STRUCTORIS.
Aº. DOMINI 1587. ÆTATIS SUÆ 40.

THE PAST

In this section we have concentrated on trying to get to know Nostradamus the man behind the myth. We have therefore included those quatrains which seem to give an insight into how he worked and what he thought and felt about his art and his talents.

He shares with us a little of how it feels and what he does as he enters his inner sanctum, his membership of a body of savants, the Rosicrucians, his feelings as he welcomes his son into his world, and his hopes as he awaits a new spiritual leader. We are privy to his world view and even look forward to the time when he is no longer trapped by his physical existence.

The latter quatrains are some of those in which Nostradamus seems to perceive a threat to the status quo in some way, whether that is the Church, government of other countries or an accepted belief. In the light of what is now known as clairvoyance, it could appear that Nostradamus sees nothing but doom and gloom. To understand this we do need to recognize that in his day and age times were hard and there was oppression around. Such a perception of travail was almost a way of life for many people in their everyday lives.

To give us some idea of how he thought, Nostradamus in his letter to his son César says:

Through this, the cycles of time –
the past, present and future –
become incorporated into one eternity

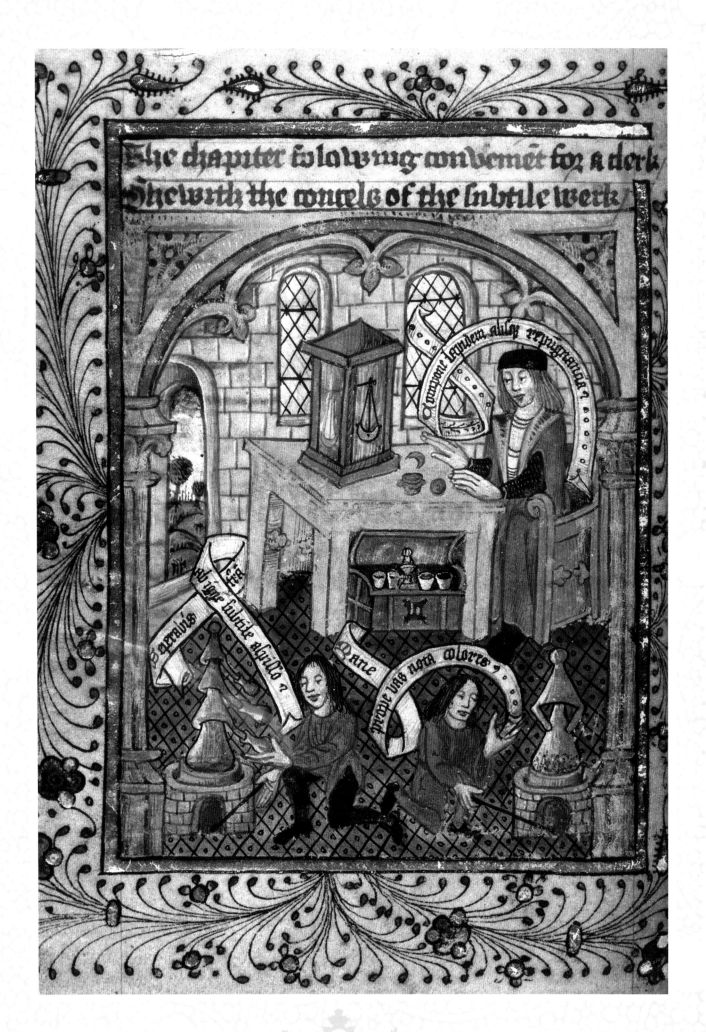

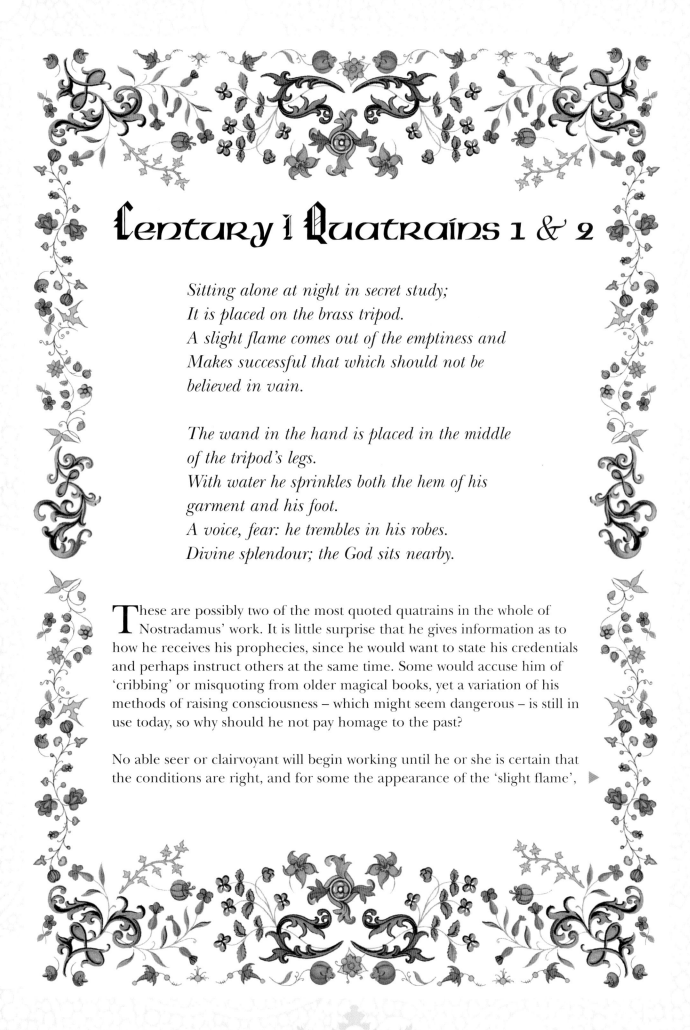

Century 1 Quatrains 1 & 2

Sitting alone at night in secret study;
It is placed on the brass tripod.
A slight flame comes out of the emptiness and
Makes successful that which should not be
believed in vain.

The wand in the hand is placed in the middle
of the tripod's legs.
With water he sprinkles both the hem of his
garment and his foot.
A voice, fear: he trembles in his robes.
Divine splendour; the God sits nearby.

These are possibly two of the most quoted quatrains in the whole of Nostradamus' work. It is little surprise that he gives information as to how he receives his prophecies, since he would want to state his credentials and perhaps instruct others at the same time. Some would accuse him of 'cribbing' or misquoting from older magical books, yet a variation of his methods of raising consciousness – which might seem dangerous – is still in use today, so why should he not pay homage to the past?

No able seer or clairvoyant will begin working until he or she is certain that the conditions are right, and for some the appearance of the 'slight flame', ▶

or perception of psychic light, is a necessary condition or precursor of those correct conditions. Many interpreters of Nostradamus' writings consider that the tripod is a holder for an alchemical flask. However, Nostradamus, who had an understanding of alchemy, would have been aware that the brass three-legged stool or tripod was an attribute of the priestly oracle known as the Branchidai (followers of Branchos) at Didyma in Asia Minor. This stool was probably used as a conductor of the subtle energies needed for divination.

A little thought will show the modern reader that this brass, combined with wet feet or a wet garment, would result in a mild electro-magnetic current, particularly if the wand were used within that magnetic current as an earthing mechanism. This reaction would cause a vibration, which could be interpreted first as what Nostradamus experiences as the 'tremble in his robes', and secondly as the spiritual voice he hears.

It would also account, through static electricity, for the physical appearance of light and also for the subjective perception of 'divine splendour'. Such a highly charged atmosphere would result in an increased heart rate, and would also give perfect conditions for looking to the future.

Nostradamus' own state of heightened consciousness would then supply the God sitting nearby, which today we would be more likely to perceive as the presence of spirit guides and helpers. Our seer would doubtless have used incenses and herbs, much as we do today, to make his vapours.

By creating the same conditions each time he worked, he would have entered into a meditative state – 'a slight flame comes out of the emptiness'. He would thus have become competent at easily accessing higher knowledge.

Century 1 Quatrain 10

A serpent's coffin is put into the vault of iron,
where seven children of the king are held.
The ancestors and forbears will come forth
from the depths of hell, lamenting to see
thus dead the fruit of their line.

This quatrain is quite fascinating. If looked at from a historical perspective, it is thought to mean among other things the extinguishing of the French royal line of Valois in the deaths of the children of Catherine de' Medici, who was a patron of Nostradamus.

If, however, it is looked at from an alchemical perspective, 'the vault of iron' is the hermetically sealed flask, an integral part of alchemy, with the 'seven children of the king' symbolizing the seven metals ruled over by the seven planets.

The 'serpent's coffin' is a symbol for one of the processes of alchemy called nigredo or 'blackening', when the bringing together of sulphur and mercury results in the 'death' of the old substances and the transformation into a new compound (mercuric sulphide). This, when refined, is known as the Golden Elixir, believed to bestow immortality.

In the last two lines of this quatrain Nostradamus thus implies that by this process of refinement, the dead, who are still trapped in 'the depths of hell', are now free, albeit with some regrets.

Century viii Quatrain 69

Close to the young one the old angel is humbled
And will come to rise above him at the end;
Ten years wandering at most the old one is
humbled again,
Of three two one, the eighth seraphim.

Without specific knowledge of spiritual matters, it is unlikely that the ordinary scholar will totally understand the meaning of this quatrain. Nostradamus has recognized, probably through his visions, that the old way of life and outdated ideas must give way to the new, and that he himself –'the old angel' – with all his knowledge, will be supplanted.

The closeness of the 'young one', presumably his son Cesar, born to him late in life, 'humbled' him and made him aware of his own mortality. He gives himself 'ten years' wandering' before he will again experience so intensely an awareness of his own world of creation. 'Three two one' is a numerological representation of the ancient Jewish Kabbalah's system of manifestation into the physical body from the spiritual realms.

'The eighth seraphim' is a representation for Nostradamus of the divine splendour of which he speaks in Century I Quatrain 2. The seraphim (plural of the word 'seraph' which means 'burn') are a class of angels considered to be higher than the cherubim, who traditionally bear the chariot of God. The seraphim's function is to burn away false doctrine and to convert man back to righteousness, a state of being dear to Nostradamus.

Nostradamus was uncannily accurate on his own behalf in this prediction, for this quatrain was probably written in 1557: he died in 1566, having given precise information elsewhere as to how he would be die – 'Ten years … humbled again'.

Century í Quatraín 27

Beneath the broken stonework of the guide from the sky
The treasure is hidden not far from there.
That which for many centuries had been gathered,
When found, decayed, the eye given credit
by its authority

This quatrain is one which we can accept as pertaining to Nostradamus' own tomb. On his death it seems he was interred at his own request in an upright position in the local church at Salon. Stories that he had had papers containing the key to all his work buried with him later proved to be untrue when the coffin was opened so that the city fathers could move the body to a better position.

Here, Nostradamus says that 'the treasure is hidden not far from there' and that what must be looked for is a piece of 'broken stonework' with perhaps a lightning symbol or angelic device – ' the guide from the sky.' Magically, this would suggest that he had at least protected his position, if not cursed those who interfered. He goes on to say that the knowledge that had been gathered 'for many centuries' will have decayed, but his clarity of vision will be given credence by the accuracy that has been shown – 'The eye given credit by its authority'.

It has to be said that no key to the conundrums that Nostradamus presents us with has been found, except through patient study and a recognition of his idiosyncracies. It does seem that time has proved him right in many of his predictions.

Century iv Quatrain 18

Some of those most lettered in the celestial facts
Will be condemned by illiterate princes:
Punished by Edict, hunted, like criminals,
And put to death wherever they will be found.

The 'celestial facts' are believed by many to mean astrologers. It is much more likely that Nostradamus intended this to mean astronomers, as in his time the two sciences were virtually inseparable.

By the time of Galileo (late 16th – early 17th century), astronomers were indeed being 'condemned by illiterate princes'. Not only were such people being persecuted by the church – 'punished by edict'– (something Nostradamus himself experienced) but they were also harassed by the secular intelligentsia.

Nostradamus was not hopeful of the new awareness and knowledge becoming available to the masses, and in his usual pessimistic fashion saw that many would be killed for their knowledge – 'put to death wherever they will be found'.

The study of Nostradamus' prophecies has itself raised an awareness of the occult in many people, and no doubt over the years has also stimulated interest in scientific theory and philosophy.

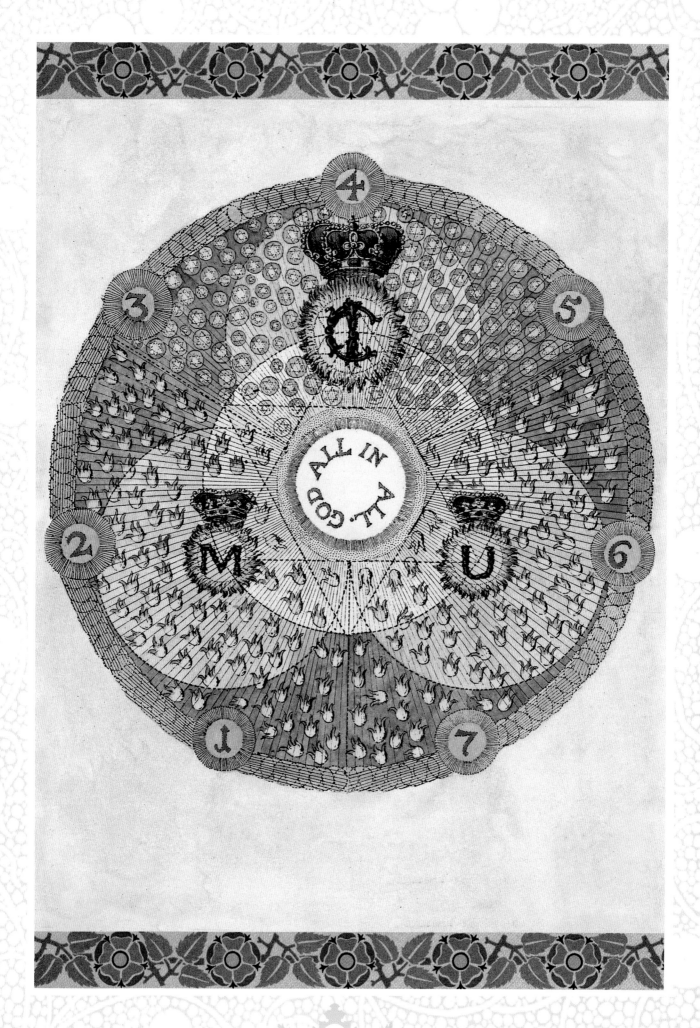

Century v Quatrain 96

The rose upon the middle of the great world,
For new deeds public shedding of blood:
To speak the truth, one will have a closed mouth,
Then at the time of need the awaited one
will come late.

This quatrain cannot be anything other than Nostradamus'
acknowledgement of the existence of (and probably his membership
of) the group of occultists and alchemists who eventually became known
as the Rosicrucians.

The rose has for some time been an alchemical representation of
spiritual transformation, which is known as the Great Work. It is also a
symbol of 'the closed mouth' (silence), necessary when dealing with
secret knowledge and truth. The cross was a symbol of the material world
– 'the great world' – and it also signified salvation after the ultimate
sacrifice, the spilling of one's life-blood. The Rosicrucian combination of
these emblems became an alchemical device used to suggest the opening
up of spiritual awareness in one whose consciousness was based in the
physical day-to-day world.

Christian Rosencreutz (1378–1484) is accepted as the instigator of the
Rosicrucians. His body, which had disappeared, was discovered by a
Brother of the Order, in a perfect state of preservation, in 1604, in a
chamber said to have been erected by Rosencreutz as a microcosm of
the universe.

This date is some 49 years after this quatrain was written, when 'at the
time of need the awaited one will come late'. Whether Nostradamus was
stating a cherished belief or forecasting the finding of the tomb, we do
not know.

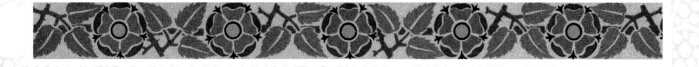

Century x Quatrain 94

Scorn from Nîmes, from Arles and Vienne,
Not to obey the Hesperian edict:
To the tormented to condemn the great one,
Six escaped in seraphic garb.

One of the greatest mistakes that can be made when trying to interpret Nostradamus is to endeavour to make him conform to time and place, and to suggest that he is actually trying to make a prophecy rather than an observation.

Though perhaps he was aware of the fact that persecution, particularly of those who thought differently from the mainstream, would become a fact of life in centuries to come, in this quatrain, he appears to be ridiculing the Spanish Inquisition, 'the Hesperian edict'. He highlights the area around Salon in France where he himself lived, an area 'from Nîmes, from Arles and Vienne,' where the Inquisition was scorned. In this way he dared to make his feelings known.

The punishments of the Inquisition, mainly directed against Jews, were conducted in public ceremonies called *autos-da-fé* (acts of faith) which frequently resulted in the burning of the victim – 'to the tormented to condemn the great one'. By using the words 'seraphic garb' Nostradamus again reveals his hidden knowledge, and suggests that six of the victims were freed from their physical bodies and revealed their true nature, that of seraphim (angels of love, light and fire).

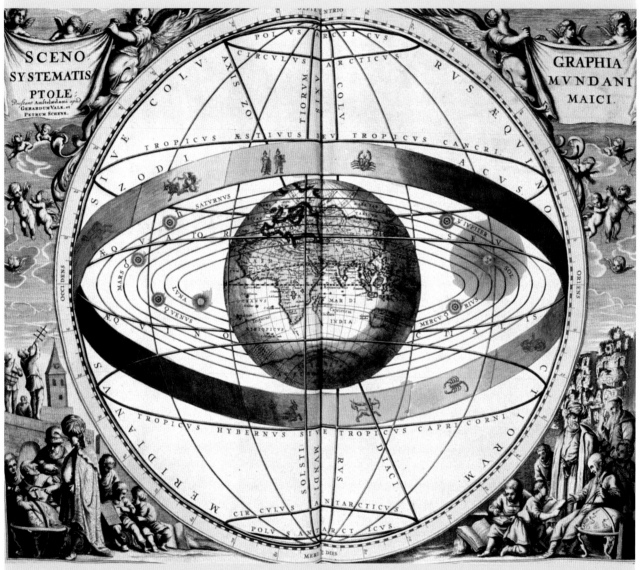

Century viii Quatrain 71

*The banding together of large numbers of astronomy
teachers will be so great,
Hounded, banished and their books censored,
In the year 1607 by sacred assemblies,
That none will be secure from the holy ones.*

For many this quatrain appears to deal with the persecution of
astrologers/astronomers. Nostradamus used the Old French word
nombre – meaning 'band of soldiers' – with reference to teachers of
astronomy, to make the point that the combined knowledge they impart
is so much of a threat to established order that they will be 'driven out,
banished and their books censored'.

He foresaw that by 1607 'sacred assemblies' would further persecute men
of science and secular society. By that time, men like philosopher
Giordano Bruno had tested accepted belief and challenged the Church's
authority. Bruno was executed as a heretic in 1600. In 1610 Galileo
published Sidereus Nuncius and shook the foundations of cosmology as
it was then understood.

Meanwhile, ecclesiastical jurisdiction had become a bone of contention
between the Church and the secular governments of various states,
particularly Venice. In April 1606 Pope Paul V excommunicated the
entire government of Venice and placed an interdict on the city – 'none
will be secure from the holy ones'.

Century 10 Quatrain 75

Long awaited he will never return
In Europe, he will appear in Asia:
One of the group issued from the great Hermes,
And he will grow over all the Kings of the East.

The Rosicrucian order was a coming together of alchemists, Christian Kabbalists and religious reformers who awaited the return of their mystical leader. 'One of the group issued from the great Hermes' is a kind of shorthand which Nostradamus has used to signify membership of this illustrious but secret organization of magicians and occultists.

Most magical practices stem from Egyptian knowledge, for the Egyptians worshipped their own gods with particular rituals designed to maximize power within the physical realm. Power over death was an important aspect of this system of knowledge. Acknowledging that the return will not be 'in Europe' but 'he will appear in Asia', Nostradamus also suggests that the returned leader will be more powerful than the Magi, the Zoroastrian 'Kings of the East' who appear in the Christmas story.

Rather than this quatrain being wholly predictive in that the leader will return, the suggestion is also that as occult (hidden) knowledge spreads, so also does power. This therefore suggests that beyond our present time there will be some kind of spiritual resurgence and a new perspective on magic.

Century í Quatraín 30

Because of the storm at sea the foreign ship
will approach an unknown port.
Notwithstanding the signs of the palm branches,
afterwards there is death and pillage.
Good advice comes too late.

Some interpreters of Nostradamus believe that this quatrain suggests a moment in our future when a space vessel touches down among us, while for others it is inexplicable. There is, however, another explanation. As always with Nostradamus, one is never quite sure how far into the future he is seeing. Here he appears to foresee an incident in French Polynesia.

In 1766 the British Admiralty officially took up the search for the Southern Continent, sending out Captain Samuel Wallis in the *Dolphin*, accompanied by Philip Carteret in the *Swallow* – an unseaworthy vessel. On entering the Pacific, bad weather – 'the storm at sea' – separated the two ships. Making for what is now known as Tahiti – 'an unknown port' – the master of the *Dolphin* noted carefully tended houses and, 'Great Numbers of Coca Nut Trees and several other trees that we could not know the name of all allong the shore', and that '… the whole shore side was lined with men, women and children all the way that we Saild allong.' ▶

On 24 June 1767, as the *Dolphin* sailed towards them, the Tahitians were thought to show hostility and Wallis replied with cannons. The next day an armed party from the ship took formal possession of the island on behalf of Great Britain, and two days later two fleets of canoes converged on the *Dolphin*, whereupon Wallis ordered the crew to fire on the approaching canoes. When the ship's guns also fired on the women and children gathered on a nearby hill the Tahitians capitulated – 'afterwards there is death and pillage'.

Some years later in the same area Captain James Cook's ship's log reports:

On approaching the shore, we could perceive with our glasses that several of the natives were armed with long spears and clubs, which they brandished in the air with signs of threatening, or, as some on board interpreted their attitudes, with invitations to land....

Captain Cook is known to have treated the people of the islands with great respect, and was initially thought to be a god. He traded with many of them for supplies, such as breadfruit, yet he himself was killed in an extremely grisly incident said to be occasioned by the greed of some of the islanders. In fact, Cook had also inadvertently transgressed some of the sacred customs of the islanders – 'good advice comes too late'?

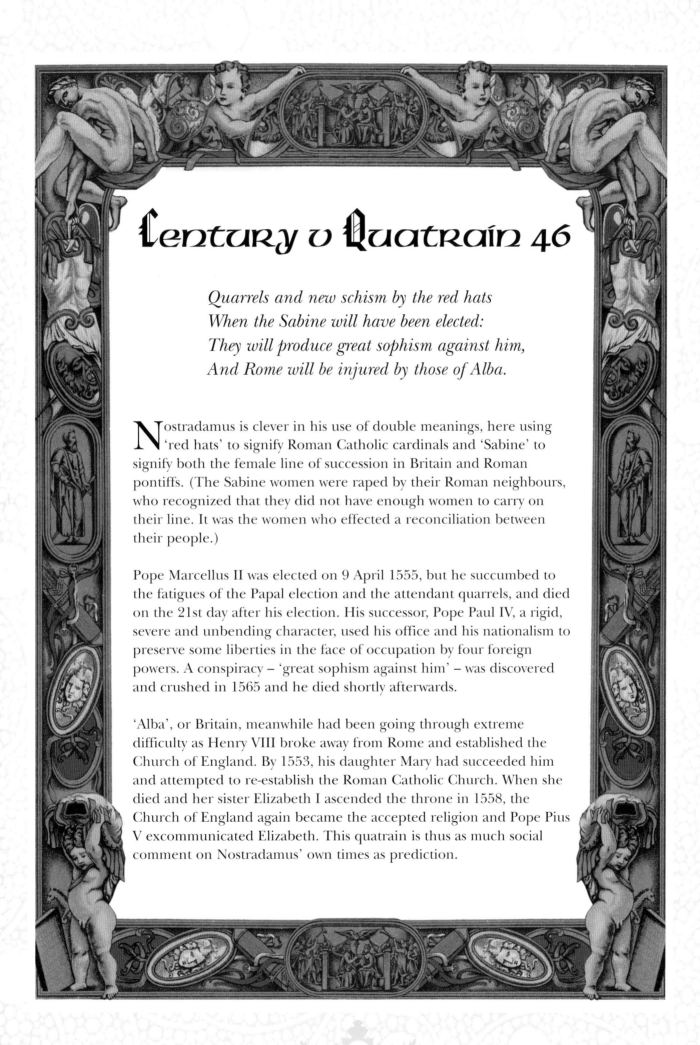

Century v Quatrain 46

Quarrels and new schism by the red hats
When the Sabine will have been elected:
They will produce great sophism against him,
And Rome will be injured by those of Alba.

Nostradamus is clever in his use of double meanings, here using 'red hats' to signify Roman Catholic cardinals and 'Sabine' to signify both the female line of succession in Britain and Roman pontiffs. (The Sabine women were raped by their Roman neighbours, who recognized that they did not have enough women to carry on their line. It was the women who effected a reconciliation between their people.)

Pope Marcellus II was elected on 9 April 1555, but he succumbed to the fatigues of the Papal election and the attendant quarrels, and died on the 21st day after his election. His successor, Pope Paul IV, a rigid, severe and unbending character, used his office and his nationalism to preserve some liberties in the face of occupation by four foreign powers. A conspiracy – 'great sophism against him' – was discovered and crushed in 1565 and he died shortly afterwards.

'Alba', or Britain, meanwhile had been going through extreme difficulty as Henry VIII broke away from Rome and established the Church of England. By 1553, his daughter Mary had succeeded him and attempted to re-establish the Roman Catholic Church. When she died and her sister Elizabeth I ascended the throne in 1558, the Church of England again became the accepted religion and Pope Pius V excommunicated Elizabeth. This quatrain is thus as much social comment on Nostradamus' own times as prediction.

Century VI Quatrain 9

In the sacred temples scandals will be perpetrated,
They will be reckoned as honours and commendations:
Of one of whom they engrave medals of silver and of gold,
The end will be in very strange torments.

Some Nostradamians feel that this quatrain relates to Napoleon and his persecution of the clergy and annexing of the Papal States at the beginning of the 19th century. Napoleon did suffer torments and indignities during his period of exile, and had medals cast which bore his image.

The quatrain could equally refer to the nefarious money-laundering activities throughout the centuries to which the Vatican seems to have turned a blind eye, and perhaps to which it has been party. It is much more likely, however, that this is Nostradamus' personal condemnation of the practice of indulgences and the striking of papal medals.

The use of blessed medals seems to have begun with the revolt of the Gueux in Flanders, in A.D. 1566, the year of Nostradamus' death, and reached a peak during Pope Sixtus V's tenure of office (1585–1590). Though he brought in many financial reforms, on his death it was obvious that his subjects hated what he had done and showed their displeasure.

The scandal associated with the Vatican Bank in the latter years of the 20th century equally fits Nostradamus' observations. The sudden and mysterious death of John Paul I and the controversy that surrounded it also fits with the words, 'the end will be in very strange torments'.

Century viii Quatrain 28

The copies of gold and silver enlarged,
Which after the ravishment were thrown into the lake,
At the discovery that all is abolished and in turmoil.
All marble out of date writings will be handed over.

In many translations this quatrain is thought to signify a future wiping out of international debt, the last line being translated as 'all scripts and bonds will be wiped out'. It is thought that 'the copies of gold and silver enlarged' represents paper money, which would have been unknown in Nostradamus' day.

It is much more likely, however, that Nostradamus perceived the looting of treasures which took place in Napoleon Bonaparte's time, when the Louvre in Paris was a scene of great activity. Numerous precious objects were moved to the Musée Napoleon after each armistice and treaty of peace. The Act of Restitution of 1815 restored most of this valuable hoard to its various owners, but Nostradamus acknowledges the antiquity of the treasures when he says 'all marble out of date writings will be handed over'.

The looting of priceless artworks and valuable antiques by the Nazi regime was another wholesale ravishment. It is only within the last few years that some of these have been returned, when original ownership has been proved – 'At the discovery that all is abolished and in turmoil' – many having found their way into various galleries and private collections in the chaotic years immediately after World War II.

One interesting footnote is that he may also refer to antiquities which have been looted from various archaeological digs around the world where their true value has not been recognized – 'thrown into the lake' – and again only those that have stood the ravages of time have been salvaged and eventually returned to their rightful owners.

Century viii Quatrain 99

Through the power of three temporal kings,
The sacred seat will be put in another place,
Where the substance of the body and the spirit
Will be restored and received as the true seat.

Nostradamus has in this quatrain foreseen the demise of the Papal States, the waning of papal secular power and the founding of the state of the Vatican City. In his day, popes had ruled a large portion of Italy for many centuries, and there is a slight note of censure, with the need to 'be restored' to a more spiritual framework.

Nostradamus' background was such that, while his family had converted to Catholicism, his knowledge was based on Jewish spirituality. When he speaks of 'the substance of the body and the spirit' he is highlighting the principle of transubstantiation, the idea that ordinary bread and wine can be changed mystically into the body and blood of Christ (a Catholic Christian belief), and spiritually can therefore be accepted as the presence of God. Where that presence is, is 'the true seat', restoring the Jewish Gnostic idea of direct experience of God.

The seer had become aware that there would be challenges to papal authority, as there were in the period from 1796 to 1798, when 'temporal king' Napoleon I invaded Italy and then demanded the renunciation of the Pope's secular authority. When that was refused, Pius VI was exiled to France –'the sacred seat will be put in another place'.

In 1861 Victor Emmanuel II became 'temporal king' of a united Italy, and annexed the remainder of the Papal States, leaving the then Pope, Pius IX, no option but to withdraw from his place of residence, the Quirinal, to the Vatican itself – 'another place'.

Finally, in 1929 (this time led by Benito Mussolini, not a king but a prime minister), disputes between a series of self-styled 'prisoner' popes and Italy were resolved by three Lateran Treaties. These established the independent state of Vatican City and granted Roman Catholicism special status in Italy – 'received as the true seat'.

Century ix Quatrain 32

A deep column of fine porphyry is found,
Inscriptions from the leaders under the base;
Bones, twisted hair, the Roman power proven,
The group is stirred at the haven of Methelin.

Nostradamus mentions the stone porphyry several times, but in this particular quatrain he is most likely referring to one of the obelisks brought to Rome by Emperor Constantine in the fourth century AD.

The Lateran obelisk was found in three pieces in Rome at a depth of 7 m, after a search by Pope Sixtus V in the former Circus Maximus. On 3 August 1588, after more than a year of effort, it was raised in the Piazza San Giovanni in Laterano, Rome, where it has stood ever since. This obelisk has inscribed on its sides Egyptian hieroglyphics – 'inscriptions from the leaders'.

Another obelisk, which now stands in the Piazza di San Pietro, was formerly on the site of the present Church of St Peter and it may be this one to which Nostradamus refers. It was removed to its present site in 1586 and does not have hieroglyphics at its base, although its site is very close to where St Peter and many other Christians were put to death – 'bones, twisted hair, the Roman power proven'.

The final line is one of Nostradamus' enigmas. The Old French may be translated, as many do, to represent 'fleet to stir at the port of Mityline', which suggests an invasion of the city of Mitilini in Lesbos, but by careful examination we can suggest the following: Methelin was known to be sleep-inducing and suggests that 'the group is stirred [i.e. alerted] at the edge of sleep'. 'The haven of Methelin' means a time when one is most likely to experience demons and nightmares, caused perhaps by the ghosts of the past, it may be that obliquely Nostradamus is admitting to some confusion.

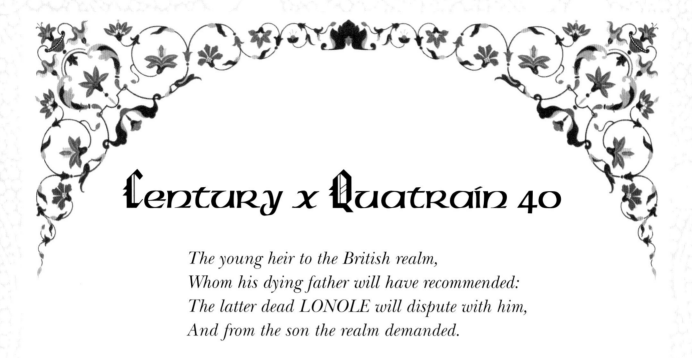

Century x Quatrain 40

The young heir to the British realm,
Whom his dying father will have recommended:
The latter dead LONOLE will dispute with him,
And from the son the realm demanded.

This quatrain is taken nowadays to refer to King Edward VIII (see also Century X Quatrain 22), and the fact that the British parliament controlled his wish to marry Wallis Simpson. This interpretation only works if we are prepared to accept conventional belief that LONOLE represents London. As we see elsewhere, however, Nostradamus usually hides something in his words written in capital letters, leaving us an enigma to solve.

British history is littered with stories of internecine wars. However, we must remember that Nostradamus was looking forward from the end of the 16th century, and it is more likely that, having seen the problems in the Tudor dynasty, he was commenting on the political machinations surrounding the death of the 15-year-old Edward VI. He had always been a sickly child, but apparently had his own agenda as to who would succeed him. Unfortunately this still leaves us with an impossible puzzle as to whom, or what, LONOLE actually is.

'His dying father will have recommended' highlights Henry VIII's obsession with the need for a male heir – he was willing to tear his country and church apart in order to fulfil this need. 'And from the son the realm demanded' would then signify those Catholics who wished to install Mary as queen and thus reinstate Catholicism as the religion of England and Wales.

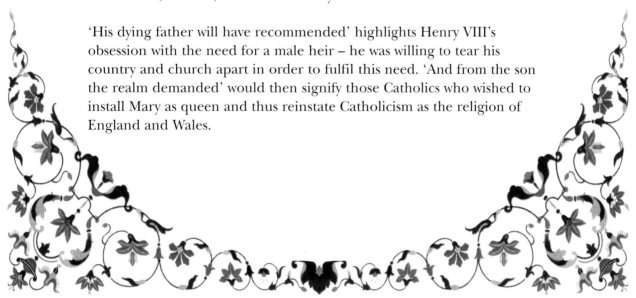

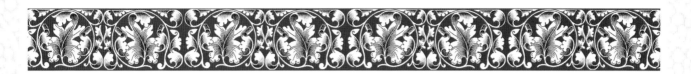

Century x Quatrain 100

The great empire will be for England,
The all-powerful one for more than 300 years:
Great forces to pass by sea and land,
The Lusitanians will not be satisfied thereby.

It is fascinating that Nostradamus foresaw the rise of England as a maritime power – 'great forces to pass by sea and land', since in his time there would seem to be little hope of such a thing happening. Inherent in the first line 'the great empire will be for England' is also the implication that England (or as we would now say, Britain) would at some point become an empire, although at the time there was no evidence of this.

The Lusitanians mean the Portuguese, who would not have been 'satisfied thereby' since they held the monopoly at that point in the exploration of new lands and colonies.

There is some controversy over the time span of 'more than 300 years' and just exactly how Nostradamus envisaged this time period, but if we take into account shipbuilding with iron, which would have confused our seer, as well as exploration, we do indeed have a time span of this magnitude, since it is only latterly that Great Britain has lost her place in the league.

What is perhaps even more surprising is that Nostradamus should have considered ending his Prophecies with such a quatrain when it was not even about his own country. There is, however, an alternative quatrain which lauds Louis XIV.

Century x Quatrain 100
alternative interpretation

When the fork will be supported by two stakes,
With six half-bodies and six open scissors:
The very powerful Lord, heir of the toads,
Then he will subject the entire world to himself.

This quatrain shows Nostradamus' ability to 'toady' to others expectations. He makes an effort here to forecast the coming of the Future King of Europe – 'Then he will subject the entire world to himself'. This man, according to Nostradamus, would have to be French and a 'very powerful Lord'.

'When the fork will be supported by two stakes, with six half-bodies and six open scissors' is said to be a representation of the Roman numerals for the year 1660. This was just a year before Louis XIV became King of France. He was indeed 'heir of the toads' in that his family's crest pictured toads, so Nostradamus identified the man correctly, if not the event. Louis XIV had absolutely no doubt of his right to rule and was known as the Sun King.

Either Nostradamus is almost trying to be too clever, since the normal representation of six is VI or he is indicating also the ultimate fate of the monarchy as it was cut down by the Revolution.

Century iv Quatrain 45

Through conflict a King will abandon his realm:
The greatest chief will fail in time of need:
Dead, ruined few will escape it,
All cut up, one will be a witness to it.

It seems most likely that this quatrain is an encapsulation of the Jacobite rebellion between England and Scotland in the period from 1685 to the uprising of 1745.

In 1688, James II of Britain 'abandoned his realm' when his son-in-law William of Orange was asked to consider ruling the country. The Whigs rallied to him; James panicked and fled the country, and was officially ruled to have abdicated – 'Through conflict a King will abandon his realm'.

Some thirty years later, the Jacobites of Scotland were similarly abandoned when the son of James II – the 'Old Pretender' as he became known – failed to arrive in time to lead a rebellion on his behalf. In reality, the whole revolt failed abysmally – principally because of the Earl of Mar's indecisive leadership. Four days after the Battle of Sheriffmuir James fled back to France, never to return – 'The greatest chief will fail in time of need'.

Bad leadership also scuppered the chances of his son the Young Pretender, Bonnie Prince Charlie, in 1745. At a point when he was within reach of victory over the English, having led his army as far as Derby, he was wrongly advised to turn back. By the time his army reached Scotland again they were tired and dispirited and at the Battle of Culloden they were trounced by the army of the Duke of Cumberland – 'Dead, ruined few will escape it'.

▶

Following this massacre, Cumberland ordered his men to execute all the Jacobite wounded and prisoners – 'All cut up, one will be a witness to it'. Cumberland became known forever afterward as 'the Butcher' because he then began a programme of reprisals which culminated decades later in the Highland Clearances when vast numbers of Highlanders were cleared off their land to make way for sheep. Many made their way to what were then called the American Colonies.

There are many frankly romantic stories afoot about what happened to the Bonnie Prince after the battle. In truth, he was completely disillusioned by what had happened, but still had hopes for a time when he would be able to recoup his losses. When his army regrouped, however, he sent a message telling his followers that every man should fight for himself. This meant that many rallied to his cause through sheer loyalty, and despite a price on his head of £30,000 he finally escaped, promising to return.

He never did however, and thus 'failed in time of need', bringing this quatrain to a full circle. His companion, Flora Macdonald, had helped him at tremendous personal risk and thus was a 'witness' to his failure. It has also been rumoured that there was a romance between Flora MacDonald and the Bonnie Prince, but it was never proven.

There is another way in which there was a witness to it, which perhaps has reverberations in the present day. Many of those who are descendants of those who chose to seek their fortunes abroad, have a tremendously romantic view of the whole saga of the Jacobite rebellion. Much of this is traceable to the historical novels of Sir Walter Scott, who wrote extensively about life in Scotland. He often highlighted the conflict between the old way of life and the new, and the whole picture of what Scotland was, and is, has come to be heavily derived from Scott's work. He has been indeed a witness to it.

In fact the Jacobite period was not a happy one for the Scots, requiring tenacity and courage simply to survive. There is still much residual resentment and anger over their treatment at the hands of the English which can surface even in today,s more tolerant times, as the move towards self government evolves.

THE PRESENT

In the area dealing with royalty, we have concentrated on British royalty of the present day, not because they are the only ones mentioned in the quatrains but because in our view they can be more clearly identified. Many Nostradamian interpreters consider that his quatrains quite clearly pinpoint the mysteries surrounding the Russian royal family and there is little doubt that the French royal family of his day are highlighted, if not always by name then certainly by nickname.

In this section we have suggested only a few quatrains which signify religious changes, pertinent to the here and now. Most more properly appear in the Future section. War and political changes play a large part in Nostradamus' perception and we can envisage his horror and puzzlement as he saw monsters that looked like iron fish and people who seemed to be setting out to destroy the world he loved. We have included several of the quatrains.

It must have been quite a task to put his quatrains together in such a way that the meaning was hidden and yet at the right time would become blindingly obvious. Nostradamus himself says in his epistle to Henry II of France:

But the injustice of the times, O Most Serene King requires that such secret events will not be made manifest except in enigmatic sentences, having however only one sense and meaning …

Century I Quatrain 96

A man will be charged with the destruction
of temples and sects, altered by fantasy.
He will be hindered by the rocks rather than living,
Hearing surfeited with embellished speeches.

This quatrain would not have made very much sense until a few years ago, though Nostradamus does comment in many of his writings on changes in religion. In the present day, as organized religions begin to change, there have arisen a number of cults and sects which can become quite fanatical in their beliefs. They can become 'altered by fantasy' in their attempts at modernization.

Nostradamus sees one man put in charge of the 'destruction of temples and sects', suggesting perhaps the need to cleanse the world of destructive ego-based beliefs. The first line can also be read, however, as 'be blamed for the destruction' and it is this meaning which has a certain poignancy today.

Until their destruction in 2001 the statues of Buddha at Bamiyan in Afghanistan were not very highly regarded. Since they were destroyed they have achieved the symbolism of icons of the destructive tendencies of the Taliban repressive government. One of the statues was 1,800 years old; the other dated from the 5th century and they are now seen as a sign of Afghan identity, more than the people themselves.

It is this that Nostradamus highlights in his comment – 'He will be hindered by the rocks rather than living.' When the focus of the world is on the destruction of what was carved out of rock, even though it is representative of long-cherished belief rather than on the plight of the people themselves, a distorted viewpoint results – 'Hearing surfeited with embellished speeches'. Necessary reforms cannot then take place and the living lose out.

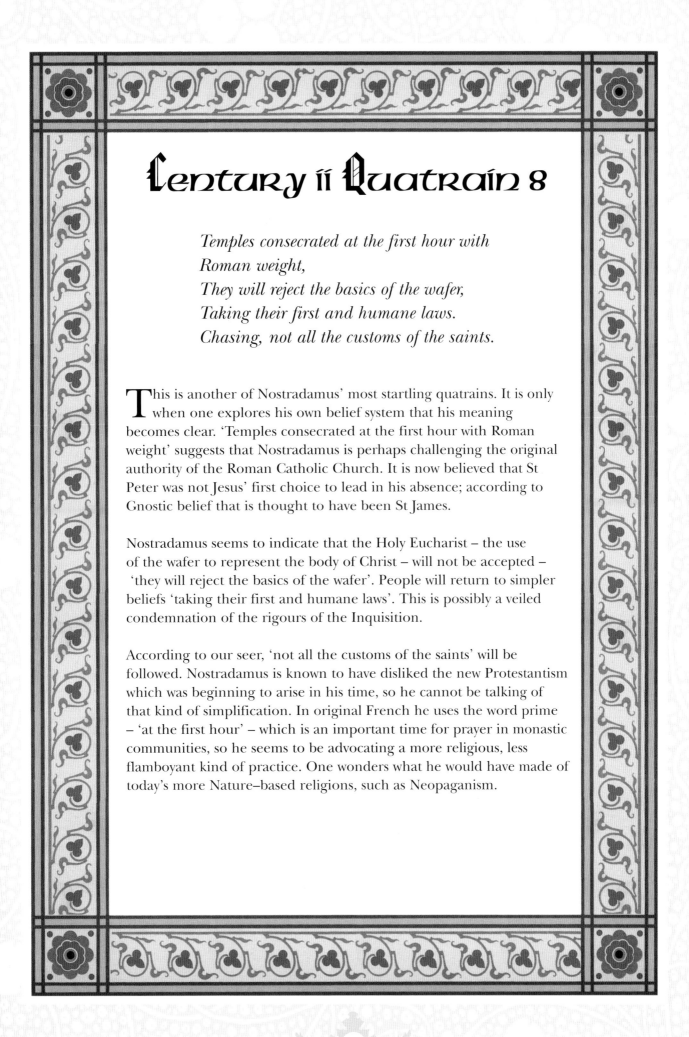

Century ii Quatrain 8

Temples consecrated at the first hour with
Roman weight,
They will reject the basics of the wafer,
Taking their first and humane laws.
Chasing, not all the customs of the saints.

This is another of Nostradamus' most startling quatrains. It is only when one explores his own belief system that his meaning becomes clear. 'Temples consecrated at the first hour with Roman weight' suggests that Nostradamus is perhaps challenging the original authority of the Roman Catholic Church. It is now believed that St Peter was not Jesus' first choice to lead in his absence; according to Gnostic belief that is thought to have been St James.

Nostradamus seems to indicate that the Holy Eucharist – the use of the wafer to represent the body of Christ – will not be accepted – 'they will reject the basics of the wafer'. People will return to simpler beliefs 'taking their first and humane laws'. This is possibly a veiled condemnation of the rigours of the Inquisition.

According to our seer, 'not all the customs of the saints' will be followed. Nostradamus is known to have disliked the new Protestantism which was beginning to arise in his time, so he cannot be talking of that kind of simplification. In original French he uses the word prime – 'at the first hour' – which is an important time for prayer in monastic communities, so he seems to be advocating a more religious, less flamboyant kind of practice. One wonders what he would have made of today's more Nature–based religions, such as Neopaganism.

Century iii Quatrain 76

In Germany will be born diverse sects,
Coming very near happy paganism,
The heart captive and returns small,
They will return to paying the true tithe.

Here Nostradamus is probably not being intentionally prophetic but is expressing his own hopes. The people of Germany, the area between the Rhine and the Danube, were known by the end of the medieval period to be very diverse in their origins, coming from Scandinavia, as well as countries to the west and east.

Nostradamus was very aware of the move in his time towards Protestantism, which he called paganism, and he fervently wished, despite the fact that his family had converted from the Jewish faith, for these diverse sects to be brought back into the Roman Catholic Church – to return to paying 'the true tithe'.

What perhaps he did not foresee in the 16th century, though his words foretell it, is the rise in the present day of the many 'sects' which now make up Paganism and Neo-paganism. These religions, in their appreciation of Nature, return to basics, and 'paying the true tithe' – originally ten per cent of all bounty received – and try to give back to the earth what they have taken from it. Even though the returns are often apparently small, when there is true commitment – 'the heart captive'– we do indeed come 'very near happy paganism'.

Century iv Quatrain 11

He who will have the government of the great cope
Will be prevailed upon to perform several crimes:
The twelve red ones who will come to soil the cloth,
Under murder, murder will come to be perpetrated.

During the Second World War, the pope, Pius XII, – 'He who will have the government of the great cope' – is now thought to have consorted with the Nazi regime; evidence has come to light that some of his policies were anti-semitic.

The 'twelve red ones' – the cardinals of the papal Curia, the ruling council of the Vatican – were known to have difficulty with the election of the next pope. They chose Angelo Roncalli, who became John XXIII, and because of his great age they assumed he would be something of a 'stopgap' pope. The cardinals reasoned that by the time this Pope died, Montini, the man they really wanted but who was not then eligible, would have become a cardinal and therefore would be eligible. (He eventually became Pope Paul VI.)

Nostradamus would have seen these machinations of the Curia as 'soiling the cloth'. Their plotting and counter-plotting may well have led to the demise in 1978 of John Paul I, who, there is now increasing evidence, was killed – 'murder will come to be perpetrated' – when he intimated that the financial affairs of the Vatican would be investigated.

Nostradamus indeed presumably both saw, and was distressed by, such negation of the spiritual duty of the popes.

Century ii Quatrain 87

After there will come from the outermost countries
A German Prince, upon the golden throne:
The servitude and waters met,
The lady serves, her time no longer adored.

This quatrain holds a great deal of interest since it is one of those which over the years has been applied to a number of reigning monarchs, not least George I of Great Britain, who brought to an end the reign of the House of Stuart.

This quatrain could equally apply to Prince Albert, consort to Queen Victoria – 'A German Prince, upon the golden throne'. One of his deliberate policies was to create a united Europe 'from the outermost countries.' It was he who saw his children as the tools with which to achieve this and encouraged sensible marriages with other heads of state.

Throughout their marriage Prince Albert acted as Victoria's private secretary and confidant on all matters. His German background worried some of the government ministers and Albert was therefore rarely consulted about political issues, though he later came to serve his adopted country well through his social conscience and farsightedness – 'The servitude and waters met.'

There were times throughout her reign when Victoria was censured by her people. Nine times pregnant, she was of necessity distanced from her subjects and during her reign there were several attempts to assassinate her. When Albert died in 1861 she went into protracted mourning and it was only when she was advised that she was losing the people's trust – 'The lady serves, her time no longer adored' – that she re-emerged into society.

Nostradamus thus once again shows his amazing perception.

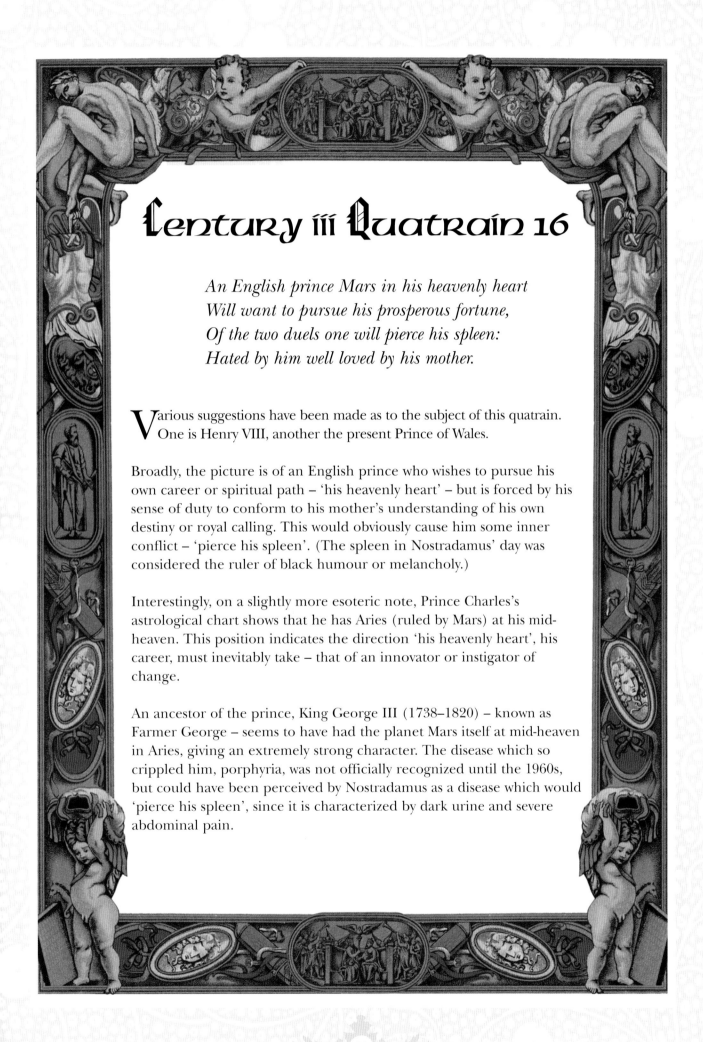

Century iii Quatrain 16

An English prince Mars in his heavenly heart
Will want to pursue his prosperous fortune,
Of the two duels one will pierce his spleen:
Hated by him well loved by his mother.

Various suggestions have been made as to the subject of this quatrain. One is Henry VIII, another the present Prince of Wales.

Broadly, the picture is of an English prince who wishes to pursue his own career or spiritual path – 'his heavenly heart' – but is forced by his sense of duty to conform to his mother's understanding of his own destiny or royal calling. This would obviously cause him some inner conflict – 'pierce his spleen'. (The spleen in Nostradamus' day was considered the ruler of black humour or melancholy.)

Interestingly, on a slightly more esoteric note, Prince Charles's astrological chart shows that he has Aries (ruled by Mars) at his mid-heaven. This position indicates the direction 'his heavenly heart', his career, must inevitably take – that of an innovator or instigator of change.

An ancestor of the prince, King George III (1738–1820) – known as Farmer George – seems to have had the planet Mars itself at mid-heaven in Aries, giving an extremely strong character. The disease which so crippled him, porphyria, was not officially recognized until the 1960s, but could have been perceived by Nostradamus as a disease which would 'pierce his spleen', since it is characterized by dark urine and severe abdominal pain.

THE EIGHT EDWARDS

Century x Quatrain 22

For not wishing to consent to the divorce,
Which then afterwards will be recognized as unworthy:
The King of the Isles will be driven out by force,
In his place put one who will have no mark of a king.

Many modern-day Nostradamians believe that this quatrain refers to the constitutional crisis that enveloped the United Kingdom in the 1930s. This involved the abdication of King Edward VIII and his subsequent marriage to an American divorcee, Wallis Simpson.

'The King of the Isles will be driven out by force' forecasts the weight of public opinion and pressure from the government that compelled him to give up his throne. His brother, George VI, was handicapped by a stammer and had not been brought up or prepared for the task of kingship – 'will have no mark of a king'.

In fact, George VI proved an able leader, winning the hearts of his subjects by his grace and dignity. He was helped enormously by his much-loved consort, who later became Queen Elizabeth the Queen Mother.

Interestingly, in Nostradamus' day this quatrain could have signified his disapproval of the actions of Henry VIII of England in using divorce to cause a schism between himself and the Catholic Church.

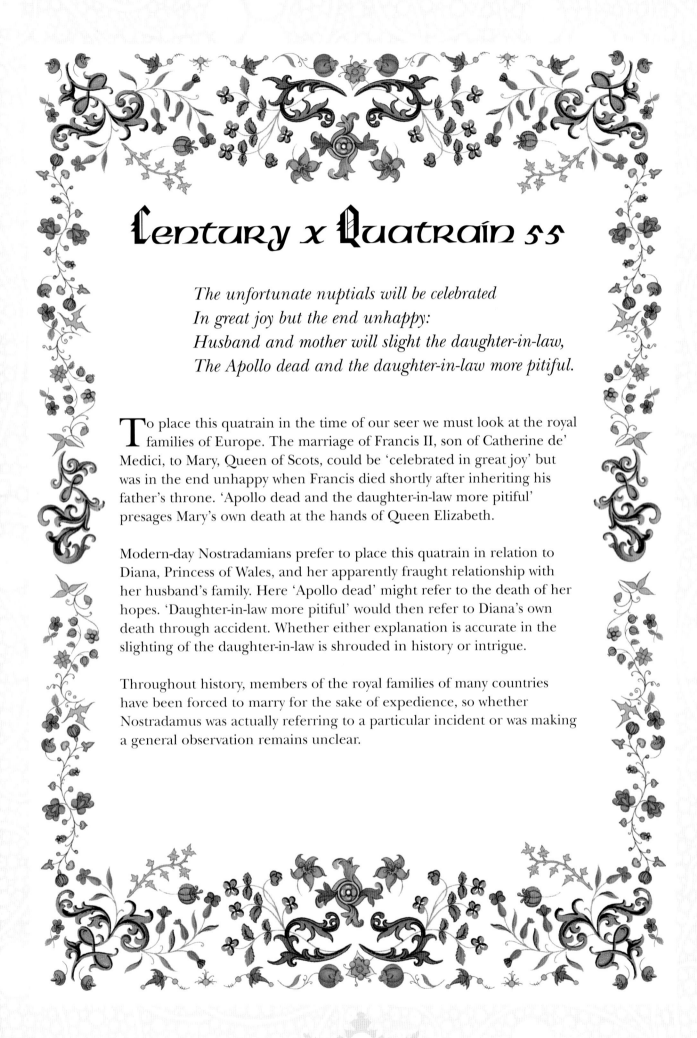

Century x Quatrain 55

The unfortunate nuptials will be celebrated
In great joy but the end unhappy:
Husband and mother will slight the daughter-in-law,
The Apollo dead and the daughter-in-law more pitiful.

To place this quatrain in the time of our seer we must look at the royal families of Europe. The marriage of Francis II, son of Catherine de' Medici, to Mary, Queen of Scots, could be 'celebrated in great joy' but was in the end unhappy when Francis died shortly after inheriting his father's throne. 'Apollo dead and the daughter-in-law more pitiful' presages Mary's own death at the hands of Queen Elizabeth.

Modern-day Nostradamians prefer to place this quatrain in relation to Diana, Princess of Wales, and her apparently fraught relationship with her husband's family. Here 'Apollo dead' might refer to the death of her hopes. 'Daughter-in-law more pitiful' would then refer to Diana's own death through accident. Whether either explanation is accurate in the slighting of the daughter-in-law is shrouded in history or intrigue.

Throughout history, members of the royal families of many countries have been forced to marry for the sake of expedience, so whether Nostradamus was actually referring to a particular incident or was making a general observation remains unclear.

Century v Quatrain 19

The great Royal one of gold, augmented by brass,
The agreement broken, war opened by a young man:
People afflicted because of a lamented chief,
The land will be covered with barbarian blood.

This quatrain is a good example of the hidden meanings within the language Nostradamus used in his prophecies. It is more than likely that the word 'barbarian' is used in its older sense, meaning 'foreign' or even in the sense of 'those who pillage' – that is, those who take that which does not belong to them.

The references to gold and brass suggest that money – probably a lack of it – is at the root of the problem of the 'people afflicted'. The 'lamented chief' might refer to a despotic and greedy ruler whose corrupt authority forces his country's economy to spiral out of control. Alternatively, this might refer to an authoritative organization that has the power to deny access to much-needed funds. In our own time we can see this happening in various parts of the world, most markedly in sub-Saharan Africa where there are difficulties with debt-relief and issues of poverty.

Nostradamus seems to expect some kind of retribution for such acts which plunge nations into penury and people into slavery.

Century v Quatrain 91

At the market that they call that of liars,
Of all Torrent and field of Athens:
They will be surprised by the light horses,
By those of Alba Mars Leo and Saturn in Aquarius.

This quatrain is one of those that make no sense unless words or punctuation are added in an effort to understand Nostradamus' own shorthand and his way of compressing his information.

'At the market that they call that of liars' may well represent the European Common Market, which later became the European Union. In spring 1999, after a scathing report suggesting corruption and mismanagement in the European Commission, the EU's governing body, all 20 commissioners were forced to step down. No one was accused of lining his or her own pockets, but they were collectively accused of having lost control of a bureaucracy that enriched others.

Whichever way one looks at it, Nostradamus seems to implicate a huge swathe of the Mediterranean basin, as far as Greece – 'field of Athens' – when he pinpoints 'all Torrent'. 'Torrent' is something of a conundrum since there are three places bearing this name, one near Valencia in Spain, another near Gerona, Spain, and the third in the Haute Savoie region of France.

Nostradamus cleverly also uses 'Torrent' in its sense of a flood as he foresees the Albanian conflict in former Yugoslavia, when many ethnic Albanians flooded into Albania from Kosovo. Also, in 2001, there was a rebellion by ethnic Albanians, those of Alba in Macedonia, that caused fears of civil war – 'Mars Leo'. Astrologically, Mars in Leo suggests aggression and the need to be in the spotlight.

'Light horses' as seen by Nostradamus most likely represent modern weapons, and it is of some concern that Saturn will be in Aquarius in March 2020. 'Saturn in Aquarius' indicates a strong likelihood of further wars in the region which was first named Albania by the Romans.

Century vii Quatrain 7

Upon the struggle of the great light horses,
It will be claimed that the great crescent is destroyed.
To kill by night, in the mountains,
Dressed in shepherd's clothing, red depths in the
deep ditch.

The 'great crescent' is usually accepted as representing the Muslim religion, and throughout history many seers and prophets have foreseen a tremendous struggle between Christians and Muslims. As yet, no claim to destroy 'the great crescent' has been fulfilled.

In the light of recent world events, this quatrain now seems to be much more specific. With its image of 'light horses' – perhaps modern missiles and armaments – it highlights the recent combative activity in Afghanistan and the Middle East.

Osama bin Laden –'dressed in shepherd's clothing' – has proved particularly elusive, because of his knowledge of the terrain – 'the mountains' – and his ability to blend into the background. The insurgents in Iraq also have this propensity to appear out of the shadows and wreak havoc, resulting in 'red depths' left by the blood of innocent victims. In a terrain so cratered by bombs, whether those of insurgents or protectors, there are inevitably 'red depths in the deep ditch'.

Whatever his faults, Nostradamus has an uncanny ability to home in on war, death and destruction, and in this quatrain he is eerily accurate.

Century viii Quatrain 64

Within the islands the infants transported,
Two out of seven will be in despair.
Those of the soil will be supported by it,
Deprived of a name, the hope of the leagues fail.

History tells us that there has until recently been a policy of child migration – 'infants transported'– within the British Isles. Ever since the early 17th century, when the first vagrant children were sent to America, there were those who 'in despair' and 'deprived of a name' had no option but to go where they were sent. Nostradamus seems to see the better side of such a policy when he says of the poor – 'those of the soil will be supported by it' – presumably bettering themselves in the process.

We can now fast forward to the years of the Second World War, and the evacuation which occurred in response to the threat of invasion of England by the Germans. Many children were sent away to the country in order to escape the expected bombing, and numerous families were traumatized by the separations. Many of the children had only known city life and found difficulty in settling into the country, particularly without parents, but those who took them in could feel that they were doing something for the war effort and be 'supported by it'. ▶

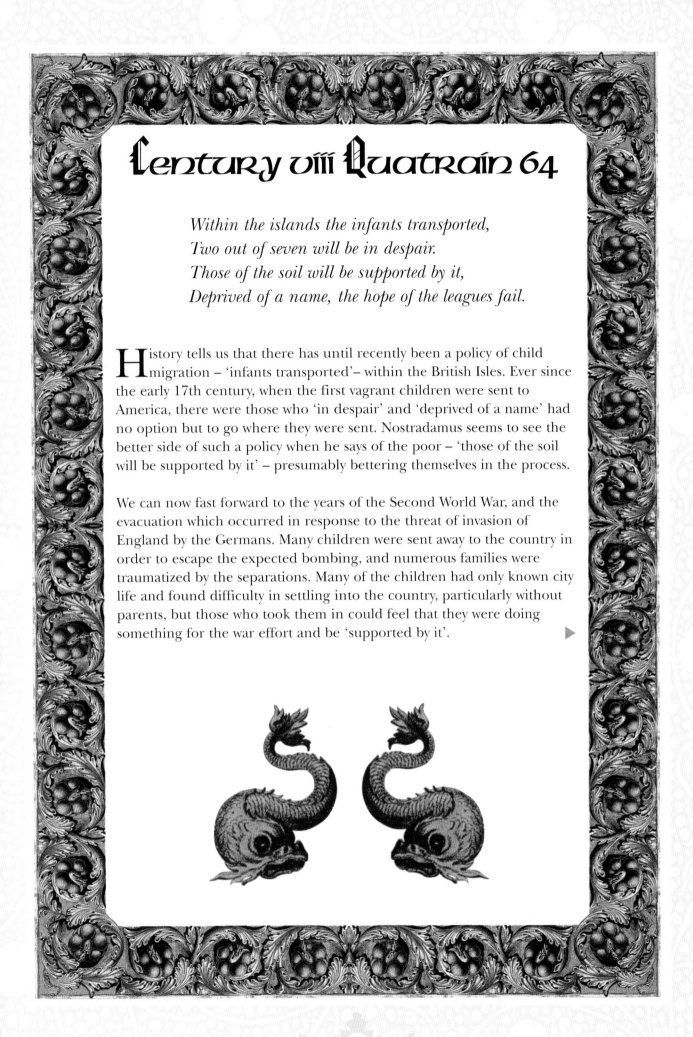

From a global perspective, shortly after the war ended the organization which was to have brought about peace to all countries, the League of Nations, was no more and had metamorphosed – 'deprived of a name' – into the United Nations Organization. To be fair, although the 'hope of the leagues' had failed, under the auspices of the League of Nations, a number of conferences, intergovernmental committees and meetings of experts were held in Geneva, in areas as varied as economic and financial affairs, health and social affairs, transport and communications, and intellectual co-operation, thus laying the foundation for some of the initiatives which still go on today.

A slightly different twist can be given to this quatrain, which means that Nostradamus was even more up-to-date in his vision. After the Second World War, the migration of children still continued to Australia, in groups varying in size from a dozen to a boatload. The children, aged between about five and 14 years, were supposedly all orphans, though this is hotly disputed, and (at least in the latter years) it was believed they were volunteers. Right up to 1963 when a halt was called, the Catholic Church Authorities in Britain were encouraged to continue sending children to Australia. Their counterparts in Australia were themselves under some pressure from the Australian government to recruit more children from the UK for migration, most likely as cheap labour. 'Those of the soil . . . '

Many of the children with no knowledge of their families, were, it is now known, abused by the very people who should have been caring for them – 'two out of seven will be in despair . . . deprived of a name'– and latterly compensation has had to be paid to many of the victims. 'The hope of the leagues fail' highlights the dereliction of duty of the organizations responsible.

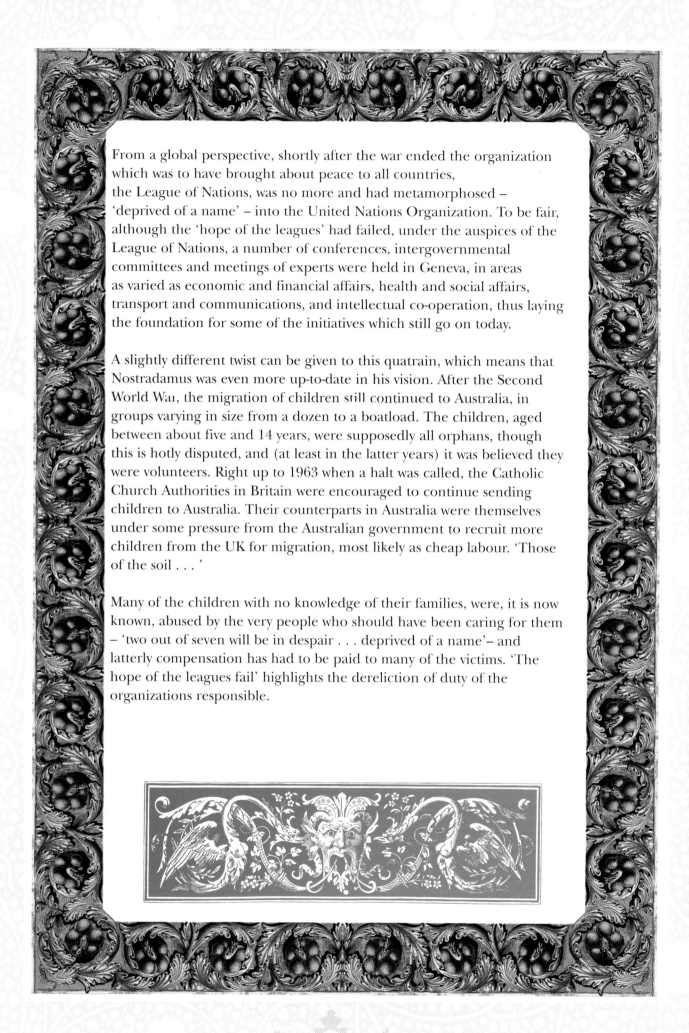

Century viii Quatrain 80

The blood of innocents, widow and virgin,
So many evils committed by means of the Great Red One,
Holy images placed over burning candles,
Terrified by fear, none will be seen to move.

Many Nostradamians suggest that this quatrain is about the Russian Revolution of 1917. 'The blood of innocents, widow and virgin' is said to represent that of the Russian royal family who were killed by the Bolsheviks. 'Holy images placed over burning candles' suggests the necessity for secrecy as the Russian Orthodox Church was forced underground. The people could not openly practise their religion for fear of upsetting the authorities – i.e. none could be 'seen to move'.

There is however a much more interesting and perhaps cosmic viewpoint which could be applied to this quatrain in the light of modern- day astronomy. The Great Red Spot, on Jupiter, is a high-pressure storm similar to a hurricane on Earth. It is massive, roughly three times the size of Earth, and has lasted for at least the 400 years that humans have been able to observe it through telescopes.

Such a phenomenon could not possibly have been observed by Nostradamus, since there were, of course, no telescopes in his lifetime. He would have perceived it as some kind of visitation by God – 'so many evils' – and extremely terrifying – 'none will be seen to move'. To someone not understanding what he was seeing it could have been a very real and present threat, since Nostradamus continually forces our perception away from the mundane.

Century ix Quatrain 7

He who will open the found tomb
And will not come to close it promptly,
Evil will come to him, and be unable to prove,
If it must be better to be a Breton or Norman King.

This quatrain is another which may be concerned with Nostradamus' own tomb, since it is on record that some 134 years after his death his tomb was opened. It is claimed that around his neck was a medallion recording the date at that time. The phrase 'evil will come to him' is thought to refer to a later occasion when his new resting place was desecrated and stories grew up of the perpetrators coming to a bad end.

However it is much more likely that this quatrain refers to the discovery of Tutankhamun's tomb in 1923 and the subsequent disasters which befell most of the participants in the dig. Although this can in no way be proved, it is now believed that the opening of the tomb after so many centuries released a bacillus, spore or virus which particularly adversely affected one of the participants, the Earl of Caernarvon. A mosquito bite on his cheek became infected, leading to his death just 47 days later. It is worth noting that within 20 years of discovering Tutankhamun's tomb, almost all of the people involved were dead, many under suspicious circumstances.

While the Earl of Caernarvon was descended from British royalty, Nostradamus seems to be suggesting that if he had been of French stock or a king, problems would have been averted – 'better to be a Breton or Norman King'.

Century ix Quatrain 14

Poisoner's cauldrons put on open ground,
Wine, honey and oil, and framed over little ovens
They will be immersed, innocent, pronounced
*   wrongdoers*
Seven smokes extinguished by the law of the limiter.

This quatrain when translated by conventional means almost defies explanation. However, if we use meanings from the ancient French, as Nostradamus often does to symbolize his ideas, we are forced to the conclusion that he has actually seen the atrocities which became known as the Holocaust.

Given that Nostradamus would have had difficulty in comprehending what he was seeing, 'Poisoner's cauldrons put on open ground' seems to suggest that whatever occurred took place away from built-up areas. 'Wine, honey and oil, and framed over little ovens' presents an image akin to cooking, which is precisely the way we now refer to those events in the Second World War when we speak of the 'gas ovens'.

Those who suffered were indeed 'innocent, pronounced wrongdoers' and the concentration camps and holding areas were numerous enough to be symbolized by 'seven smokes'.

Finally, Hitler could indeed be called 'the limiter', as he attempted to exterminate the Jews and produce the perfect Aryan specimen.

Century x Quatrain 97

Triremes full of captives of every age,
Good time for bad, the sweet for the bitter:
Prey to the Barbarians hasty they will be too soon,
Anxious to see the feather wail in the wind.

Triremes were boats with three banks of oars first seen in ancient Greece. We might make a leap of faith and suggest that Nostradamus used the word to describe what now we would call a cruise liner. 'Full of captives of every age' would be his perception of those who travelled below deck as being incarcerated in some way.

'To see the feather wail in the wind' could suggest the combination of a ship's hooter and the plume of smoke from a ship's funnel, again a modern-day image. This quatrain has a sense of disaster about it, highlighting action which is too precipitate – 'hasty they will be too soon.'

There are persisting rumours that in 1915, the *Lusitania*, a luxury liner which was sunk by a German submarine in May of that year, was carrying munitions as well as passengers across the Atlantic – 'good time for bad, the sweet for the bitter'.

The deaths of many American citizens in the disaster was considered to be contrary to international law and the conventions of all civilized nations, and caused America to take more of an interest in the war in Europe. 'Prey to the Barbarians' could refer to this, the Barbarians being the Germans.

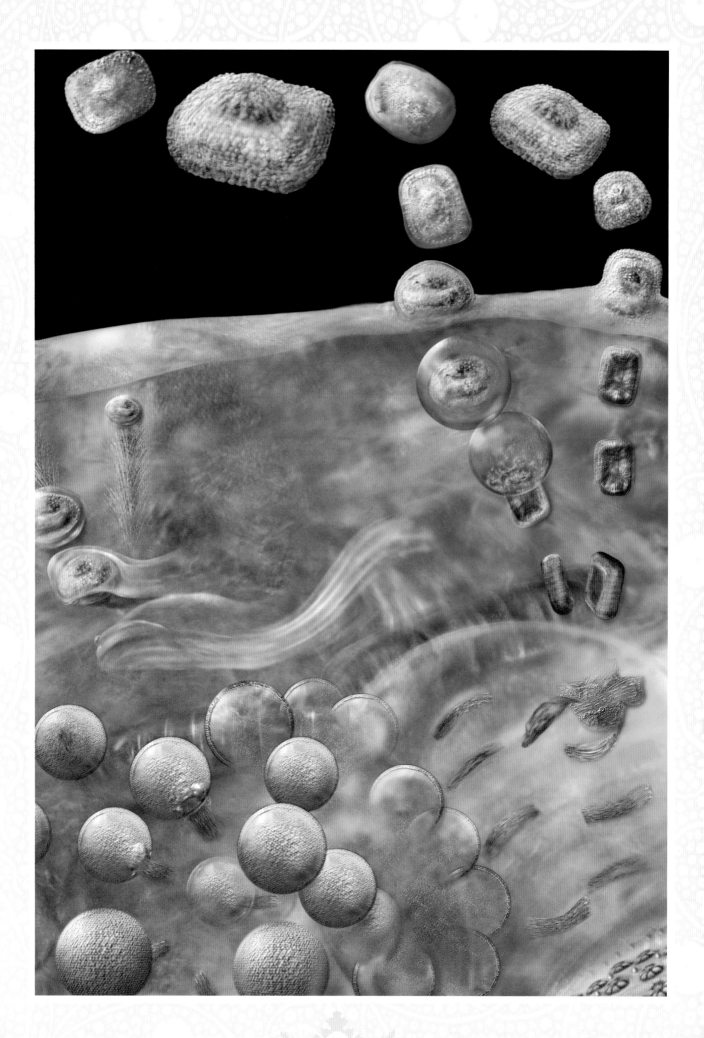

Century 1 Quatrain 25

The lost thing is discovered, hidden for many
centuries.
Pasteur will be celebrated almost as a God-like figure.
This is when the moon completes her great cycle,
but by other rumours he shall be dishonoured.

This quatrain is generally taken to suggest that Nostradamus actually named Louis Pasteur as having rediscovered ancient knowledge when he discovered that germs pollute the atmosphere.

Pasteur became one of the founders of modern science and microbiology and would teach his disciples: "Do not put forward anything that you cannot prove by experimentation." Having been feted for his breakthrough, he then fell from grace when it was discovered that, during his work on the anti-rabies vaccine before a full trial had been undertaken, a Joseph Meister's mother appealed to Pasteur to treat her son who faced death having been bitten repeatedly by a rabid dog. Pasteur, against his own principles, treated the boy, who fortunately recovered.

Along with Edward Jenner, Pasteur also developed the smallpox vaccine in an effort to rid the world of a scourge of its time. Recent reports indicate that there are moves afoot to modify the smallpox vaccine genetically as a first line of defence against possible terrorist attack, surely a misuse of Pasteur's healing principles – 'by other rumours he shall be dishonoured'.

Interestingly, the Pasteur Institute was opened in 1887 which coincided with the end of the 'Age of the Moon' – 'the moon completing her great cycle'. This, by calculation, had begun in 1535, just prior to the time of the *Prophéties*.

There is however an equally valid interpretation, just as stunning in its accuracy. The Old French word 'Pasteur' translates as 'shepherd' and in 1945 at Nag Hammadi in Egypt a peasant unearthed that which indeed had been 'hidden for many centuries': ancient texts which were to challenge the world's view of Early Christianity.

Unfortunately the discoverer did not fully realize what treasure he had found. Many of the texts were burned as fuel and ridiculed as he was, 'by other rumours he shall be dishonoured'.

Century i Quatrain 92

Under one man peace will be proclaimed everywhere,
but not long after will be looting and rebellion.
Because of a refusal, town, land and sea will be
broached.
About a third of a million dead or captured.

This quatrain holds particular significance in the modern day and could be applied to the situation in Iraq. It is particularly pertinent in that Saddam Hussein brought a form of peace to his country, albeit through autocratic rule – 'under one man'. His people however became progressively impoverished, while he, his family and cohorts prospered.

'Because of a refusal'– not allowing UN weapons inspectors to discover whether he possessed weapons of mass destruction, his country was invaded – 'town, land and sea will be broached' – and in the aftermath many were killed or taken prisoner. At the time of writing the situation is still unresolved, though Saddam Hussein and many of his associates have been captured.

'Looting and rebellion' now goes on as insurgents oppose efforts by American and British forces to bring peace to the region. The total number of 'dead or captured' – 'a third of a million' – may well be surpassed before the end of conflict.

Some Nostradamus interpreters suggest that this quatrain could be attributed to wars closer to his own time and may have its roots in prophecies prior to that. In some of his other quatrains Nostradamus also forecasts a short-lived peace, without specifying where this takes place.

Century í Quatraín 29

When the fish that travels over both land and sea
is cast up on to the shore by a great wave,
its shape foreign, smooth and frightful.
From the sea to the walls the enemies soon come.

Century íí Quatraín 5

Who inside a fish, surrounded by iron and letters,
Out will go one who will then make war,
He will have his fleet well rowed by sea,
Appearing near the Latin land.

It is well established that students of Nostradamus suspect that he tended to rework prophecies by other seers, an invasion by Muslim forces being one of them. As so often happens, we have been given no real time frame in which to operate, yet in both these prophecies Nostradamus appears to be seeing something at least 400 years ahead of his time.

Both these quatrains speak of amphibious or sea vehicles, whether hovercraft, landing craft or submarines, and of enemies which come from the sea – 'from the sea to the walls the enemies soon come'. The startling aspect of these visions is the picture they engender for the reader.

There is no way that Nostradamus could have any concept of a fish-shaped vessel made of iron which could travel over land and sea, and yet his graphic descriptions conjure up a picture of a submarine or an amphibious vehicle, which could belong to the Second World War, the Gulf Wars, or to some future conflict.

Nostradamus indicates in the second quatrain that a 'fleet' – i.e. more than one such vessel – will appear and then land somewhere on, or near, the Italian coast. This latter quatrain may be an attempt to meld together what he sees in his visions and what he has learned from other soothsayers.

THE FUTURE

The quatrains in this section largely fall into two areas. We have entitled the first subsection Extreme Conditions, and included in this extreme weather and famine and pestilence. Nostradamus does not like what he sees and it is hardly surprising. The sun no longer warms, it boils the fish in the sea. There is drought, hardship and a scarcity of resources. He, who had studied the human condition, measured the stars and tried to alleviate human suffering, had already lost members of his own family to the plague, and his heart must have sunk as he realized the gargantuan task which would face humanity.

The second part of our study of the future is perhaps more hopeful. The quatrains that we have chosen from the *Prophéties* allow the reader to survey the possible changes in religious thought that take place. We have also sought out some of the quatrains that in our view are alchemical and therefore transformative in their intent. The reader can then move forward into new exploration.

Nostradamus does not see the end of the world quite yet and perhaps we all can even now take the time to redeem ourselves and create a better future for our world and its inhabitants.

Nostradamus in his letter to Henry II says:

However, I was hoping to leave a written record of the years, towns, cities, regions in which most of the events will come to pass ... beginning from the present time which is the fourteenth of March 1557, and passing far beyond to the coming advent which will be after the commencement of the seventh millennium ...

Century 1 Quatrain 67

The great famine which I sense approaching
will often turn then become worldwide.
It will be so vast and long lasting that one will grab
roots from the trees and children from the breast.

Century 1 Quatrain 69

The great mountain, seven stadia round,
after peace, war, famine, flooding.
It will spread far, drowning great countries,
as well as antiquities and their mighty foundations.

One of the ways in which Nostradamus hides information is to give it in random order, almost as though he has picked up numerous pieces of paper and shuffled them. Many people have tried to rearrange his quatrains, to work out his anagrams and to uncover the code that he uses to hide his information. These two quatrains are exceptional in their accuracy and are there for us to interpret easily, unfortunately only after the event.

Nostradamus does not exactly specify volcanic disaster as such in these quatrains, although he speaks of the great mountain spreading. He seems to concentrate on the aftermath of such a disaster.

To make sense of both of these quatrains we have to change the order in which we read them and take 69 first. In this he speaks of a huge mountain 'seven stadia round' – which is equivalent to a circle of about 300 metres in diameter – 'drowning great countries as well as antiquities and their mighty foundations'. This must make it a mountain of water, which strongly suggests the tsunami or tidal wave which occurred during the writing of this book at the end of 2004.

Turning then to quatrain 67, Nostradamus gives warning of the famine which he 'senses approaching'. At this present time there is already famine in various parts of the world, and there is the sense of the problem growing 'so vast and long-lasting' that it cannot be properly dealt with, but keeps returning, so that the sufferers must 'grab roots from trees' and stop feeding their babies.

When we put the information Nostradamus gives us in these two quatrains together, we have the foretelling of a natural disaster which is so huge in its implications that it does not bear thinking about. Some seers have forecast a natural or man-made disaster in the Mediterranean basin, but recent events would suggest that these particular quatrains specify somewhere else.

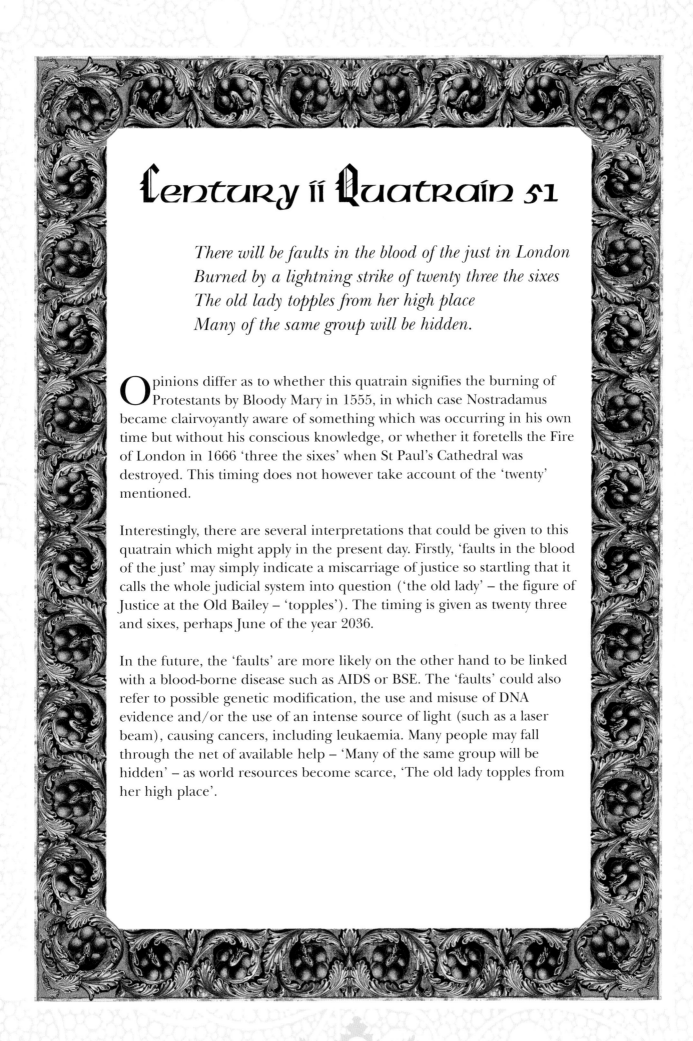

Century ii Quatrain 51

There will be faults in the blood of the just in London
Burned by a lightning strike of twenty three the sixes
The old lady topples from her high place
Many of the same group will be hidden.

Opinions differ as to whether this quatrain signifies the burning of Protestants by Bloody Mary in 1555, in which case Nostradamus became clairvoyantly aware of something which was occurring in his own time but without his conscious knowledge, or whether it foretells the Fire of London in 1666 'three the sixes' when St Paul's Cathedral was destroyed. This timing does not however take account of the 'twenty' mentioned.

Interestingly, there are several interpretations that could be given to this quatrain which might apply in the present day. Firstly, 'faults in the blood of the just' may simply indicate a miscarriage of justice so startling that it calls the whole judicial system into question ('the old lady' – the figure of Justice at the Old Bailey – 'topples'). The timing is given as twenty three and sixes, perhaps June of the year 2036.

In the future, the 'faults' are more likely on the other hand to be linked with a blood-borne disease such as AIDS or BSE. The 'faults' could also refer to possible genetic modification, the use and misuse of DNA evidence and/or the use of an intense source of light (such as a laser beam), causing cancers, including leukaemia. Many people may fall through the net of available help – 'Many of the same group will be hidden' – as world resources become scarce, 'The old lady topples from her high place'.

Century II Quatrain 75

The voice of the rare bird heard,
On the pipe of the air-vent floor:
So high will the bushel of wheat rise,
That man will be eating his fellow man.

In many religions birds are thought to represent the soul, and are also often seen as foretelling danger or disaster. The image of the call of the 'rare bird' is a potent one, for the phoenix, the most famous of fabulous birds, is said to have a melodious voice that becomes mournful with approaching death.

In this quatrain Nostradamus seems to hear an eerie sound like that of air blowing across an empty pipe, perhaps that of a modern empty warehouse or grain store. He indicates there is a shortage, 'so high will the bushel of wheat rise', and the price of grain becomes so inflated that some will have to resort to cannibalism in an effort to survive – 'man will be eating his fellow man'.

Many of Nostradamus' quatrains forecast doom and gloom, but this one is especially disturbing, particularly as famine becomes more prevalent in the Third World. We see in other quatrains the effect that the mismanagement of resources has had in these countries and around the world.

Century ix Quatrain 55

The horrible war which is being prepared in the West,
The following year will come the pestilence
So very horrible that young, old, nor beast,
Blood, fire Mercury, Mars, Jupiter in France.

Recent experiences of pestilence such as SARS and avian flu render this quatrain eerily accurate. When Nostradamus speaks of 'the horrible war which is being prepared in the West', he does not necessarily mean war as such, but war in the sense of a fight against sickness. He himself had already lost a wife and children to a particularly nasty form of the plague, so he knew only too well how quickly such disease could spread.

Today, infectious diseases can spread even faster due to international air travel, and Nostradamus foresees that neither 'young, old, nor beast' will be exempt. By using the symbolism of Mercury, Mars and Jupiter he signifies that communication, war and economic expansion (three attributes of the planets according to astrological belief) will be the ways in which disease is spread.

Perhaps without intending to he also intimates the part that France plays in the fight against diseases such as AIDS, through world-renowned bodies such as the Pasteur Institute.

Century ix Quatrain 83

Sun twentieth of Taurus the earth will tremble
very mightily,
It will ruin the great over-filled theatre:
To darken and trouble air, sky and land,
Then the non-believer will call upon God and saints.

Because Nostradamus had knowledge of both astronomy and astrology, he was able to pinpoint with a fair degree of accuracy where the sun will be 'twentieth of Taurus' when this earthquake 'will tremble very mightily'. The only problem is that he does not tell us the year in which it will happen.

When Nostradamus wrote of a 'great over-filled theatre' he could not have known about the huge football and games stadia which are built in the present day. Unless his words refer to the amphitheatres of the ancient world, it is most likely one of these which will be most affected by the earthquake to which he refers. In Great Britain, the Hillsborough tragedy took place on 15 April 1989, when many football fans were killed as a result of an overfilled stadium. However, the timing is not quite correct, so we must put this quatrain in our future.

It seems that the catastrophe Nostradamus perceived will be so great that 'the non-believer will call upon God and saints'. This suggests that it will be sufficient to test the faith of those who normally claim to be agnostics or atheists. Nostradamus here forecasts a time when air, sky and land will be darkened and troubled and once again seems almost to enjoy being the bearer of unpleasant news.

Century iii Quatrain 34

When the obscuring of the Sun will then be,
In full daylight the oddity will be seen:
Quite otherwise will one interpret it,
No allowance against high prices nothing will have
been provided there.

This particular quatrain seems to speak of an eclipse of the sun – 'the obscuring of the Sun' – concurrent with which are perhaps strange cloud formations or light effects – 'the oddity will be seen'.

Remembering that in Nostradamus' day such things would have been seen as omens or portents, he suggests that the 'oddity' defies description and will be interpreted in the wrong way. There will, it seems, be problems in supplying the necessities of life, and measures which would avert danger and difficulty will not have been taken.

The total eclipse of the sun in 1999 did not show the 'oddity' Nostradamus feared, nor so far as we know has any other. One is therefore left with the feeling that perhaps he was perceiving something far more dangerous – perhaps a nuclear explosion, or another cataclysmic event such as the burning out of a meteorite – which might obscure the sun, thus causing worldwide economic and practical difficulties.

Century ix Quatrain 48

The great city of the maritime Ocean,
Surrounded by a crystalline swamp:
In the winter solstice and the spring,
It will be tried by frightful wind.

It has been suggested that in this quatrain 'the great city of the maritime Ocean' may represent Shanghai, as it becomes the financial capital of Asia. It could, however, also be any city which consists mainly of glass buildings. 'Surrounded by a crystalline swamp' might also place it in an icy region, or indeed in some future scenario.

There are, at this present time, signs that large bergs of ice are breaking away from the main floes due to global warming and climate changes. The next line – 'in the winter solstice and the spring' – gives precise times of year when we need to be concerned, and a time window which should be identifiable. The last line forecasts gales and other such mighty winds – 'it will be tried by frightful wind'.

At the same time as global warming and climate changes seem to be taking effect and the seasons become more unpredictable, we also have developed new building techniques which allow our buildings to reach unprecedented heights. There is more and more risk to those who must use such buildings, and the 'terrible wind' may be trouble still to come as we learn to value properly the planet on which we live.

Century III Quatrain 90

The great Satyr and Tiger of Hyrcania,
Gift presented to those of the Ocean:
A fleet's chief will set out from Carmania,
One who will take land at the Tyrren Phocaean.

Most interpreters of Nostradamus are agreed that this quatrain signifies Iran, but again we must try to get inside Nostradamus' mind to ascertain exactly what he saw. He frequently used mythology and animals to signify a country or area, and this stanza is full of such symbolism.

The Satyr in mythology was a Greek sylvan deity or demigod, represented as part man and part goat, and characterized by lecherous behaviour. The national animal of India traditionally is the tiger, so, according to our seer, here we have an alliance between 'those of the Ocean', possibly Greece or other Eastern Mediterranean countries, and India. This places the affiliation very firmly around the Caspian Sea in an area once known as Hyrcania. Nostradamus would not have known that this area is extremely oil- and gas-rich, commodities or a 'gift' much needed by India.

At the time of writing, a potential route for an oil pipeline has been proposed, through Iran and on to Turkey, identified in this quatrain as 'Tyrren Phocaean', the area now known as West Anatolia. Nostradamus tells us that the principal port of export – 'A fleet's chief will set out' – or the starting point for the 'gift' will be Carmania, an ancient Iranian name for the Strait of Harmuz. Only time will tell if he is right.

Century vi Quatrain 35

Near the Rion and close to the white wool,
Aries, Taurus, Cancer, Leo, Virgo,
Mars, Jupiter, the Sun will burn a great swathe
Woods and warnings letters hidden in the candle.

Most Nostradamians suggest that 'Rion' signifies the constellations of Ursa Major and Minor, but it could equally indicate that of Orion, which would have been just as well known to our seer. Nowadays we have the use of powerful telescopes and can see clearly the Great Orion Nebula, located in the 'sword' part of the constellation of Orion, just below the most easterly of the three stars that comprise Orion's belt. It has been observable since antiquity, but its true nature would not have been known until telescopes were invented, after Nostradamus' time. Is this perhaps the 'white wool' that Nostradamus sees with his inner eye?

He then goes on apparently to blame this phenomenon for a climate disaster lasting from March to August – 'Aries, Taurus, Cancer, Leo, Virgo' – when 'Mars, Jupiter, the Sun' will be acting in unison to create either forest fires or desert. This does not necessarily mean that the planets are conjunct (together in the sky), simply that their aspects (the angles between them) cause conflagration.

It seems that in the last line, 'woods and warnings letters hidden in the candle', Nostradamus gives us some idea of how he has received his information. By the use of incense and by staring at a candle he has revealed again something of which he could not have been aware consciously.

Benedictolus Rubei Massini.

Lucduicus Arloti.   de Dorf S Petri.

Century í Quatrain 4

In the universe there will be made a King
who will have little peace and a short life.
At this time the ship of the fishers will be lost,
governed to its greatest detriment.

It is now widely believed that Nostradamus was echoing a medieval seer, St Malachy of Ireland, in this quatrain. St Malachy had, along with others, forecast the demise of the papacy in a time not too distant from our own. He had, while in trance, listed the names of every pope there was to be, and according to this list there are only two to come after the present one, John Paul II.

While most translations speak of the 'world', Nostradamus in his original uses the word *univers*, which we can take in its original meaning of the known universe. This then would suggest that there will be one ruler (or perhaps an all-pervading principle) which will bring a short-lived peace to the world as we know it.

It is suggested that at that time the Catholic Church – often symbolized by others as the barque of St Peter, the fisher of men – will lose its supremacy due to the way it is being governed. As alternative ways of thought become more prominent, perhaps the Gnostic idea of direct experience of God becomes more feasible and there will be less need for organized religion.

Century v Quatrain 31

Through the Attic land fountain of wisdom,
At present the rose of the world:
The bridge ruined, and its great pre-eminence
Will be subjected, a wreck amidst the waves.

The 'Attic land' is the area around Athens which thus signifies Greece and the seat of democracy, which in Nostradamus' day would have been considered 'the rose', or the most highly principled centre of the world.

Nostradamus here highlights the struggles of the peoples of the Balkan peninsula north of Greece for autonomy and freedom. In particular, this quatrain concentrates on what has become known as 'the Former Yugoslav Republic of Macedonia'. Macedonia, in ancient times, was under the rulership of Alexander the Great, the pre-eminence of which Nostradamus speaks about.

After declaring its independence from the Socialist Federal Republic of Yugoslavia, following a referendum in September 1991, the republic became involved in a dispute with Greece over its official name. The Greek government then put a trade embargo on it, which had a devastating impact on the country's economy.

Macedonia was cut off from the port of Salonica and became landlocked – 'the bridge ruined' – because of the UN embargo on Yugoslavia to the north, and the Greek embargo to the south. Macedonia has never fully recovered its economic equilibrium, and it is now much less of a power – 'a wreck among the waves'.

Century v Quatrain 41

Born in the shadows and during a dark day,
He will be sovereign in realm and goodness:
He will cause his blood to rise again in the ancient urn,
Renewing the age of gold for that of brass.

This is one of our seer's most enigmatic pronouncements. It is thought by some to forecast the coming of a new leader for the French people, who would go on to rule the world. Francis II was born in 1544 during a solar eclipse. He married Mary, Queen of Scots, in 1558, and thus became king of Scotland.

He was set to be 'sovereign in realm and goodness', and did indeed become king of both France and Scotland on the death of his father, Henri II. While elsewhere in the *Prophéties* Nostradamus accurately predicted that several of Catherine de' Medici's children would rule France, he does not here seem to have foreseen Francis' early death in 1560.

In another completely different interpretation, Nostradamus acknowledges his own profession as seer and foretells the coming of a New Age, which we now call the Age of Aquarius – 'the ancient urn'. A highly evolved spiritual leader, born during an eclipse, will deal with the materialism of our present time and bring about a new awareness of spirituality. (Brass was often used as a conductor in spiritual communication –'renewing the age of gold for that of brass'.)

Thus Nostradamus may be expressing a fervent hope for his country, or foreseeing the present-day rise in interest in his own prophecies and the pursuit of hidden knowledge.

Century ii Quatrain 70

The dart from the sky will make its extension,
Deaths in speaking great execution.
The stone in the tree the proud nation restored,
Noise human monster purge expiation.

The image which is called to mind by this quatrain is that of the Tower in the tarot which suggests a kind of internal cleansing of a given structure by a thunderbolt sent from the heavens. The whole point of this is that the world as we know it is turned topsy-turvy, and what was once normal no longer is. Not understanding what he saw might also lead Nostradamus to see a radio, or mobile telephone, mast in such a way.

A subsidiary interpretation is equally hopeful. If 'the stone' is taken to represent the Islamic Ka'aba, the Holy Stone of Mecca, and 'the tree' to be the cross of the Christians (which is often known as the Tree), when the two faiths come together with a common purpose – 'the stone in the tree' – although there will be much initial protest, there will also be a cleansing of malevolence, hatred and misunderstanding – 'the proud nation restored'.

'The dart from the sky' may well be some kind of communication device which initially appears to bring death and destruction with it, but ultimately is a force for good. Much of the previous fighting between nations will achieve peace – that is, 'expiation'.

It is worth noting that Nostradamus frequently confuses us by his lack of punctuation. However, in this case, he leaves us to read the last line as we see fit and makes no judgement as to the rights and wrongs of what he feels.

Century 111 Quatrain 2

The divine word will give to the substance,
Including heaven, earth, gold hidden in the mystic milk:
Body, soul, spirit having all power,
As much under its feet as the Heavenly see.

Nostradamus occasionally gives us glimpses of the ways in which he receives his information. In this quatrain he talks of 'the divine word', clearly suggesting the vibration of which he speaks in Century I Quatrain 2. 'The substance' is the realm of physical being, and he is conscious of the fact that in an enlightened state – 'body, soul, spirit having all power' – he has access to knowledge including that which is hidden from normal perception in the spiritual realms – 'the mystic milk'. That knowledge in alchemical terms is the power of manifestation, the ability to create 'gold', or make things happen.

It seems also that he recognizes the visionary nature of the information he receives, and the sense of power that occurs when he is entranced. He plays with words here, so that those who have not experienced an extreme state of heightened spiritual consciousness first-hand will have no concept of what it actually feels like.

Experiencing what today we call the Void (what the Chinese call *wuwei* or nothingness) gives one a sense of vastness, a sense of everything being somewhat distanced – 'under its feet'– a feeling similar to that we would imagine is experienced by God on His heavenly throne as he surveys his Creation.

Century vii Quatrain 41

The bones of the feet and the hands restrained,
For a long time the house is inhabited by clamour
Pressures unearthed through dreams
The house healthy is inhabited without noise.

Many Nostradamians believe that this quatrain is connected with some kind of exorcism of a haunted house, but in fact the house referred to is much more likely to be a symbol of the personality. Modern psychology accepts that dreams create symbols of security. The house is one such easily identifiable image. Nostradamus seems to have been ahead of his time in recognizing that the house represents the self, so this quatrain becomes a healing technique which uses dreaming as a therapy.

It is not totally clear whether Nostradamus intended 'the bones of the feet and the hands restrained' to be a directive for others or a reason for his own 'house inhabited by clamour'. There are many ancient Eastern meditative techniques which suggest, as part of quietening the mind, making a circle with the thumb and third finger of each hand and placing the soles of the feet together, as though closing a circuit. We do not know for certain that Nostradamus had conscious knowledge of this technique, yet the picture he presents would suggest so.

As one becomes more competent in meditation the dreams can become more vivid and reveal past traumas and difficulties – 'pressures unearthed through dreams' – until, with the return of full health, the mind becomes tranquil – 'inhabited without noise'. Nostradamus in his spiritual quest seems to have had access to advanced knowledge and was well aware of the results of both mental stress and sensitivity.

Century viii Quatrain 90

When those of the cross are found their senses troubled,
In place of sacred things he will see a horned ox,
Through the virgin the pig's place will then be filled
Order will no longer be maintained by the king.

Nostradamus again sets out in this quatrain to confuse us, but equally he expects us to follow his symbolism, which is based on a knowledge of the Kabbalah and Egyptian magic.

By 'those of the cross' Nostradamus means Christians, and he suggests that when they cannot make sense of their faith they return to ancient beliefs. 'A horned ox' was a representation of the God of Israel in pre-Christian times, when he was known as the Bull-headed One. Egypt had previously chosen this animal to represent God, and bull worship became prevalent in the ancient world.

With this awareness, one comes to understand the true meaning of the virgin birth as a power for redemption. 'Through the virgin the pig's place will then be filled', and evil will be conquered (in the Jewish faith the pig is unclean). Nostradamus then suggests that power will no longer be held by a secular monarch – 'no longer maintained by the king'.

It has been suggested that from a worldly perspective this quatrain speaks of the power of Islam and the potential for an Arab invasion. If this were so, then it would be more likely to be a clash of beliefs than an actual military invasion.

Century IX Quatrain 12

So much silver of Diana and Mercury,
The images will be found in the lake:
The sculptor looking for new clay,
He and his followers will be steeped in gold.

This quatrain is one of Nostradamus' alchemical quatrains. When he refers to 'silver of Diana' he reveals his knowledge that in alchemical terms silver was named after the moon, because of its white lustre. Diana is the goddess of the moon.

Nostradamus indicates that mercury and silver are brought together in a process designed to convert baser metals into gold – not necessarily true gold, but in the production of 'the Elixir of Life'. This elixir in Nostradamus' time was thought to give the alchemist the ability to re-create man in his own image – 'the images will be found in the lake'. Nostradamus suggests that almost as a by-product of this process – 'the sculptor looking for new clay' – gold will be produced in excess. 'He and his followers will be steeped in gold.'

There is a tendency nowadays to link any mention of Diana in Nostradamus' quatrains to the late Diana, Princess of Wales. We should give credit to Nostradamus for knowing his mythology, which enabled him to conceal some of his true meanings in such references.

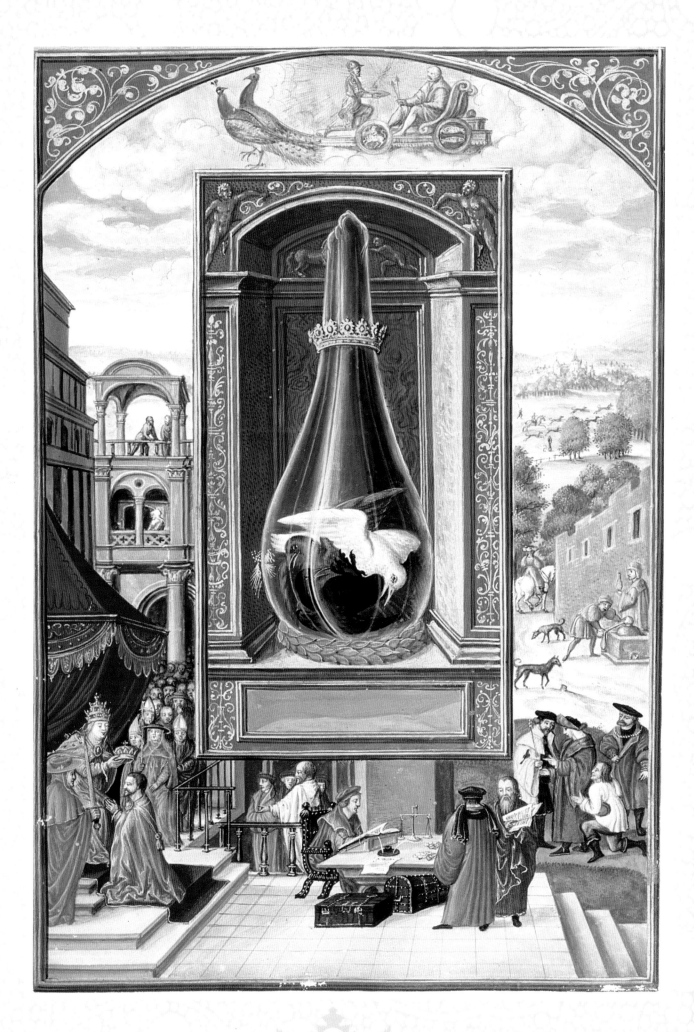

Century iv Quatrain 33

Jupiter joined more to Venus than to the Moon
Appearing with white fullness:
Venus hidden under the whiteness of Neptune
Of Mars struck by the carved branch.

While many would wish to read this quatrain as pertaining to the planets, since Neptune was not discovered until 1846 it is unlikely to be so. If, however, we read the quatrain in alchemical terms we perhaps can get a little closer to Nostradamus' record of his workings.

If we remember that alchemists would work with salts and solutions of metals, this quatrain sounds more like a recipe, or instructions, for those in the know. Each planet has a metal assigned to it. Tin (the metal of Jupiter) combined, it seems, more successfully with copper or brass (Venus) rather than with silver (Moon) and resulted in a salt 'appearing with white fullness'.

This resulting metallic salt was then 'hidden under the whiteness of Neptune'. This suggests that it was dissolved in pure water (Neptune is the God of the sea) within an iron (Mars) flask. This was then 'struck by the carved branch' – one assumes his wand or a specially shaped holder, presumably in the same way as homeopathic remedies are made today.

It is a pity that we do not know the outcome of this experiment, and to give Nostradamus his due, he is remarkably generous in recording it. On the other hand, he may have been using symbolism to hide what he was doing from prying eyes.

Saturne Cibelle

Jupiter

pluto venus

Juno

Cy parle des ymages
et figures que les anchiens
assignoyent aux dieux. Et
premiers de saturne ..

Ous denons oul
tre encores seconde
ment entendre
que les anchiens
des dits entre lesquelz ceste

Century v Quatrain 24

The realm and law raised under Venus,
Saturn will have dominion over Jupiter:
The law and realm raised by the Sun,
Through those of Saturn it will suffer the worst.

This quatrain has been given many meanings over the years, but it is one of those which can only really be fully understood in terms of alchemy. This states that certain metals are ruled by 'the realm and law' of planets. Venus' metal is copper, Saturn's is lead and Jupiter's is tin.

Alchemy sets out to refine baser metals and turn them into gold, the metal of the Sun. Nostradamus seems to be offering advice on the order of working the various metals, but he admits that the manufacture of gold is inhibited by lead, one suspects through contamination.

Bearing in mind that alchemy also symbolizes the refinement of the soul on its journey to perfection, Nostradamus warns that 'those of Saturn' who are basest in their make-up can seriously impede 'the law and realm raised by the Sun' – the search for truth. Our seer is perhaps taking a side-swipe at those who hounded alchemists in his day, but he also issues a serious warning to those who, in our times, search for spirituality. They may 'suffer the worst'.

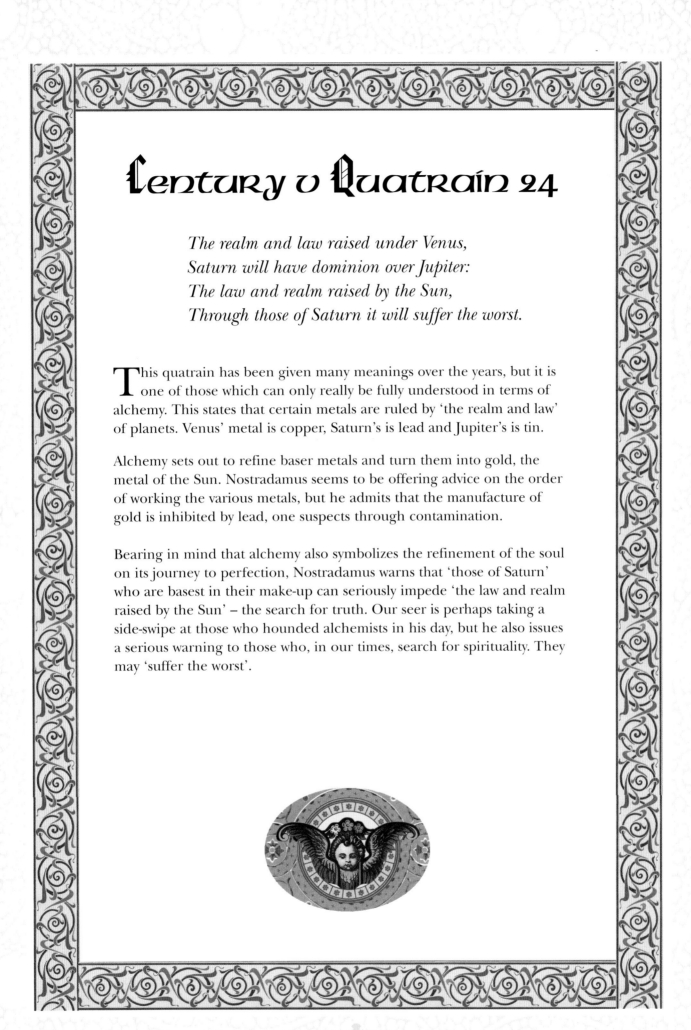

Incantation Of The Law Against Inept Critics

Let those who read this verse consider it profoundly,
Let the profane and the ignorant herd be not drawn:
And far away all Astrologers, Fools and Barbarians,
May he who does otherwise be subject to the sacred rite

Traditionally placed between Centuries VI and VII, this quatrain is often taken to be directed against critics of Nostradamus' work. In fact, it is much more of a warning to those who have not fully developed the critical faculty of objectivity or clarity of vision. Our seer asks that anyone who reads further must think carefully about what they do – 'Let those who read this verse consider it profoundly'. He protects his work not by a curse but by an incantation which requests that 'the profane and ignorant herd' (non-believers in the arts he practises) are not even interested in his work.

Those who are mere 'Astrologers, Fools and Barbarians' – that is, beginners, dabblers and Non-Christians – must also be barred from full understanding. Nostradamus indicates that he has performed some kind of ritual – 'sacred rite' – to protect his work and therefore unless the reader has undergone some form of initiation, whether privately or otherwise, he or she will not be entirely privy to the information which our seer provides.

Certainly, experience suggests that anyone who sets out to interpret the latter quatrains in Nostradamus' work does have to penetrate some kind of mental obstacle before coming to the conclusion that the task becomes simpler if one treats the work from a more esoteric viewpoint.

In the spirit of Nostradamus' warning therefore we would caution those who would mock the interpretations which have been given in this book. As was suggested in the introduction, often the meanings of the quatrains become clearer if one 'sits with them' and lets the meaning become gradually apparent. If Nostradamus achieved his objective of seeing things which are divine as well as human, he was also a past master at giving us riddles to solve and conundrums to unravel. Perhaps even he could not have foreseen the longevity of some of his perceptions, though he did write in his letter to his son:

'They are perpetual prophecies and extend from now to the year 3797.'

If the reader's understanding of the quatrains does not fit in with the more conventional explanations, then so much the better; it means that there is fresh knowledge to be had even in the present day. For many years people have looked retrospectively for proof that he was right and as always it is easy to be wise after the event – to say 'Ahh that was what he meant!' The chances are that what he wrote about has – and will – come to pass in ways that even he could not have envisaged, since the world has changed so much since his time.

In conclusion, we offer two quotes for your consideration. One is from the Holy Bible and is from Proverbs 20:12

'The hearing ear and the seeing eye, The Lord has made even both of them'

The second is from Nostradamus himself, who says in his letter to Henry II:

'For the chronology which follows agrees little if at all with that which is superior, although as much was seen by astronomy as by other sources, including the Holy Scriptures and cannot be wrong.'

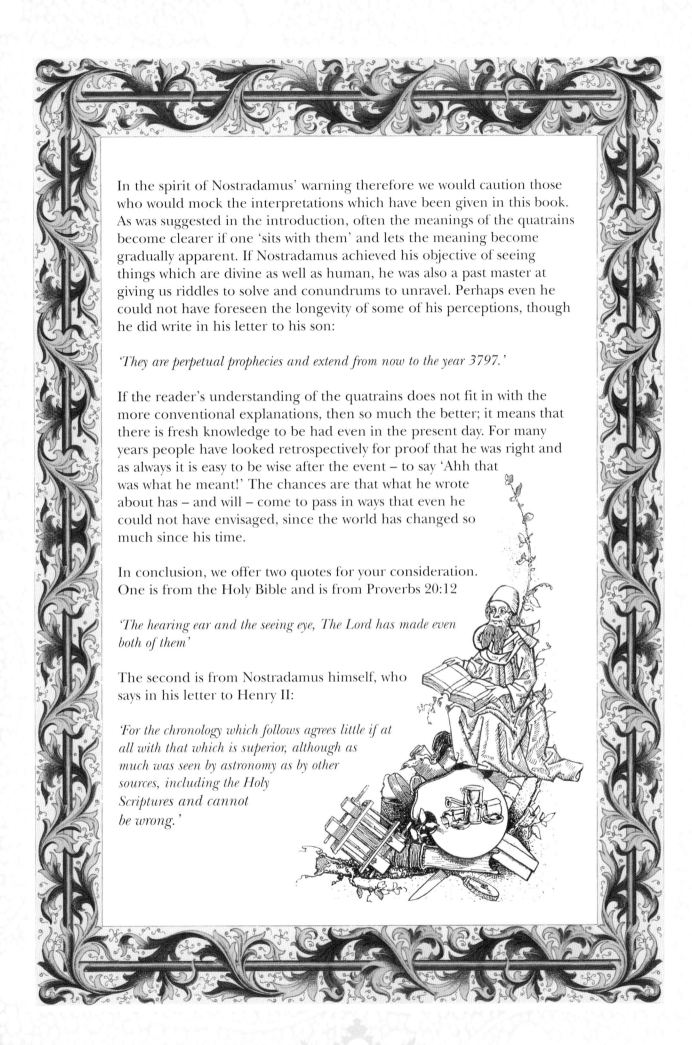

Picture credits

P10 Tycho Brahe (1546-1601) Danish astronomer, in his observatory, from 17th century Atlas by Blaeu [The Art Archive/Maritiem Museum Prins Hendrik Rotterdam/Dagli Orti]

P12 Alchemists preparing experiments for distillation in search of gold from *Ordinal of Alchemy* by Thomas Norton English c.1490 [The Art Archive/British Library]

P15 From *Splendor Solis* ('The splendor of the sun'). Man climbing a ladder leaning against a fruit tree, 1582. [TopFoto.co.uk (c) The British Library/HIP]

P16 From *Splendor Solis* ('The splendor of the sun') Alchemist with a flask, 1582 [TopFoto.co.uk (c) The British Library/HIP]

P18 Seraph mosaic 12-13th century Byzantine [The Art Archive/Basilica San Marco Venice/Dagli Orti]

P20 Historical artwork of a lightning strike [Shiela Terry/Science Photo Library]

P22 Northern Celestial chart by Thomas Hood 1590 [The Art Archive/John Webb]

P24 Plate 13, Vol 1 *The Works of Jacob Behmen, The Teutonic Theosopher,* [Topfoto.co.uk]

P26 *Members of the Inquisition from auto da fé presided over by Saint Dominic* [The Art Archive/Museo del Prado Madrid/Dagli Orti]

P28 Ptolemaic system of the Universe, 1708 [TopFoto.co.uk HIP/Ann Ronan Picture Library]

P30 *The Bird of Hermes* from 'Ripley Scroll' [TopFoto.co.uk]

P32 *Point Venus, Island of Otahytey,* 1792, Tobin, Captain George (1768-1838)/Mitchell Library, State Library of New South Wales/www.bridgeman.co.uk

P35 Captain Cook eating with Tahitians engraving [The Art Archive/Musee des Arts Decoratifs Paris/Dagli Orti (A)]

P36 *Hersilla throwing herself between Romulus and Tatius,* 1645, Guercino [akg images/Erich Lessing]

P38 The Pope in council – illustration to the *'Decretum' of Gratian of Chiusi* [Mary Evans Picture Library]

P40 *The Four Ages of Life, The Iron Age* [The Art Archive/Palazzo Pitti Florence/Dagli Orti (A)]

P42 *The Fortress of Faith* [Mary Evans Picture Library]

P44 Fontana dei Quattro Fiumi [John and Lisa Merrill/Corbis]

P46 Edward VI [Mary Evans Picture Library]

P48 Britannia [Mary Evans Picture Library]

P50 *Triumph of King Louis XIV of France driving the Chariot of the Sun,* Werner, Joseph (1637-1710)/Chateau de Versailles, France, Lauros/Giraudon/www.bridgeman.co.uk

P52 *A Lost Cause, Flight of King James after Battle of the Boyne* [The Art Archive/Tate Gallery London}

P55 Charles Edward Stuart and Flora McDonald [Mary Evans Picture Library]

P56 Kronos supporting the vault of the heavens [The Art Archive/Palazzo Reale Madrid/Dagli Orti]

P58 *The Creation of the World,* icon, late 18th century Russian [The Art Archive/Roger Cabal Collection/Dagli Orti]

P60 Novices receiving communion and unction, from *Redemption Triptych* [The Art Archive/Museo del Prado Madrid/Dagli Orti]

P62 Pan by a stream [Mary Evans Picture Library]

P64 Voting for Pope [Mary Evans Picture Library]

P66 Queen Victoria with Albert and children [Mary Evans Picture Library]

P68 Lancelot and Tarquin [Mary Evans Picture Library]

P70 Edward VIII and Edwards [Mary Evans Picture Library]

P72 Marriage ceremony and preparation for adoption of children fresco by Domenico di Bartolo 1443 [The Art Archive/Santa Maria della Scala Hospital Siena/Dagli Orti (A)]

P74 *The Miser's Treasure,* Flemish School, (17th century)/Musee des Beaux-Arts, Valenciennes, France, Lauros/Giraudon/www.bridgeman.co.uk

P76 Leo from *Calendar and Book of Hours,* French mid 15th century [The Art Archive/Bodleian Library/The Bodleian Library]

P78 *Peace* [www.bridgeman.co.uk]

P80 Sailing ship under full sail [Mary Evans Picture Library]

P83 *Liverpool Docks* [Mary Evans Picture Library]

P84 Aurora over Jupiter [Science Photo Library]

P86 Tutankhamun Tomb [Rex Features]

P88 *Hell,* from The Last Judgement [The Art Archive/Stadtmuseum/Dagli Orti]

P90 *The Ship of Odysseus,* Schmied, Francois-Louis (1873-1941)/ Private Collection/www.bridgeman.co.uk

P92 Smallpox virus life cycle [Russell Kightley/Science Photo Library]

P94 Hanging Gardens of Babylon [Mary Evans Picture Library]

P96 Underwater operation against battleship [The Art Archive/Museo Storico Navale Venice/Dagli Orti (A)]

P98 Diving for gold, Wray, General E.W. (1823-92)/www.bridgeman.co.uk

P100 Armillary sphere [The Art Archive/Private Collection Paris/Dagli Orti]

P102 *The Tree of Life* [The Art Archive/Museo de Zacatecas Mexico/Dagli Orti]

P105 Artwork of a tsunami [Lynette Cook/Science Photo Library]

P106 *Fleeing the Great Fire of London* [Getty Images]

P108 Phoenix arising from the flames from *Bestiary* [The Art Archive/Bodleian Library Oxford/The Bodleian Library]

P110 The Planet Mars, from the manuscript of the *Spheres* [The Art Archive/Biblioteca Estense Modena/Dagli Orti (A)]

P112 Roman amphitheatre, Nimes, France [The Art Archive/Bibliotheque des Arts Decoratifs Paris/Dagli Orti]

P114 Solar Eclipse [Getty Images]

P116 Passage through the ice [The Art Archive/Navy Historical Service Vincennes France/Dagli Orti]

P118 Sagittarius from *Breviary of Ercole of Este* [The Art Archive/Biblioteca Estense Modena/Dagli Orti]

P120 *The Path of the Sun through the Stars,* detail of Orion and Taurus [Pesello, Giuliano d'Arrighi (1367-1446)/www.bridgeman.co.uk

P122 St Peter meets Christ [The Art Archive/Biblioteca Augustea Perugia/Dagli Orti (A)]

P124 Alexander the Great enthroned [The Art Archive/Bodleian Library Oxford/The Bodleian Library]

P126 Aquarius from the *Signs of the Zodiac,* Jordaeans, Jacob (1593–1678)/Palais du Luxembourg, Paris, France, Giraudon/www.bridgeman.co.uk

P128 Building the Tower of Babel, from the *Bedford Book of Hours* [The Art Archive, British Library]

P130 King David of Israel and God [The Art Archive/Bibliotheque Mazarine Paris/Dagli Orti (A)]

P132 Mandala of Primordial Buddha [The Art Archive/Lucien Biton Collection Paris/Dagli Orti]

P134 Taurus from *Calendar and Book of Hours,* French mid 15th century [The Art Archive/Bodleian Library Oxford/The Bodleian Library]

P136 *Luna,* Burne-Jones, Sir Edward (1833-98), The Maas Gallery, London, UK/www.bridgeman.co.uk

P138 From *Splendor Solis* ('The splendor of the sun") Three birds in a flask/British Library, London, UK/www.bridgeman.co.uk

P140 *Olympus with Saturn, Pluto, Juno, Venus, Jupiter and Cybele* French School 15th century/Bibliotheque Nationale, Paris, France, Giraudon/www.bridgeman.co.uk